In Corridors of Eternal Time

In Corridors of Eternal Time

A Passage Through Grief

A JOURNAL

ဆ • ශ

JANICE GRAY KOLB

Blue Dolphin Publishing

Published by Blue Dolphin Publishing, Inc.
P.O. Box 8, Nevada City, CA 95959
Orders: 1-800-643-0765
Web: www.bluedolphinpublishing.com

ISBN: 1-57733-135-4

First printing, November, 2003

Library of Congress Cataloging-in-Publication Data

Kolb, Janice E. M.
    In corridors of eternal time : a passage through grief : a journal /
Janice Gray Kolb.
        p. cm.
    ISBN 1-57733-135-4 (pbk. : alk. paper)
    1. Kolb, Janice E. M. 2. Pets—Death. 3. Grief—Miscellanea. 4. Cats.
5. Bereavement—Miscellanea. I. Title.

BF1997.K65A3 2003b
155.9'37—dc22
                                                                2003015769

A portion of any profits realized by sales of this book will be used to support
various animal charities.

Photos and sketches by the author.
Cover photo of the entry road to the cottage as seen by Rochester daily.

Printed in the United States of America

10   9   8   7   6   5   4   3   2   1

Dedicated
to my
beloved feline
soulmate
Rochester

and

to my
beloved
husband and soulmate
Bob

and

to Rochester's and my
spiritual friend
Chris Comins
who is a blessing and strength
through this passage

It Is Such A Secret Place—the land of tears
—Antoine deSaint Exupery (1900–1944)

i carry your heart with me (i carry it in
my heart) i am never without it (anywhere
i go you go, my dear; and whatever is done
by only me is your doing—
—e.e. cummings.

In the essential of what they meant to us,
the dead live on with us as long as we ourselves live.
Sometimes we can speak to them and take counsel of them
more readily than with the living.
—Hermann Hesse

Contents

Rochester
January 2002

A Word in Preparation

WHEN A HUMAN WE LOVE DIES, we feel the impact and terrible desolation that accompanies that separation. We feel empty and distraught because the sweet presence of that loved one will no longer be a part of our lives. We realize with an overpowering certainty that the quality of our own lives has suddenly become less. We as individuals have become diminished because the lifescape that was once enhanced by a loved presence is no longer complete. I share the author's feeling of loss in the passing of a very special cat named Rochester.

If the passion of a consuming love is directed toward an animal, the results will be the same as toward a human. The void created by that absence can be just as complete. Our response to death does not depend on where human society places that individual on a chart of animal worth, but where you as an individual, place him as a participant in your own life. It's dealing with the intensity of your love, the degree of your involvement with the lost one, and the changes that will be forced upon you by that individual's absence that may dictate the parameters of your grief.

Many of us, when contemplating or trying to come to grips with the reality of death, believe that the passing of a presence does not mean the annihilation of a spirit. The unfathomable mystery of eternity and all that it implies is more than we can comprehend. Despite our cognitive limitations in achieving an understanding of what occurs after death, we believe that Heaven exists and that there will be a reuniting with those that we have loved here on earth.

In facing the reality of the author's loss of her beloved Rochester who was her friend, pet, and companion, she has presented here her raw and candid emotions and reactions as they actually happened and were felt. Her journey down this difficult road is presented here in such a way that you will vicariously feel a part of her experience, and by so doing, find strength for your own dealings with the death of your animal companion.

Robert A. Kolb, Jr.
June, 2002

Acknowledgments

May the words of this book—and the meditation of our hearts
(the readers' and mine)—give glory to God—
all glory to my Christ—
and love and gratitude to Blessed Mother Mary—
who always intercedes.

℘ • ℆

I wish to thank my
Guardian Angel
and my special Angels
who are ever present

℘ • ℆

I wish to express my extreme appreciation to Paul M. Clemens, Publisher of Blue Dolphin Publishing, for believing in this book and for his kindness and grief support and to all his capable staff who helped in so many ways. I especially thank Chris Comins, Linda Maxwell, Jeff Case, Jody Black, and Barbara Houtchens for their fine work and their friendship.

℘ • ℆

I wish to thank Rochester for his constant love, presence, devotion, inspiration, and teachings throughout our life together. Because of him this book was written.

❧ • ☙

I am deeply grateful to my husband Bob for his love and support, for believing in me, and for our life together in New Hampshire. I am grateful too for the time he gave in endless hours typing this manuscript.

❧ • ☙

I wish to thank
St. Francis of Assisi
and
St. Martin dePorres
for their great love and protection of all God's creatures

❧ • ☙

A Tribute In Gratitude

—for Rochester

"Whatever enchants, also guides and protects. Passionately obsessed by anything we love—an avalanche of magic flattens the way ahead, levels rules, reasons, dissents, bears us with it over chasms, fears, doubts."
—Richard Bach, *The Bridge Across Forever*

Only yesterday from the carton he pushed his tiny head
And I—in giddy inner joy realized he was mine.
By this golden-eyed precious being I have been led—
Into wondrous knowledge of creature love divine.
The bond that has deepened connecting us soul to soul
Has enriched my very life and made me whole.
Never can I again be as I was before—
Knowing all I now know—taught me by him whom I adore.
I hear God speak through my loving companion—in silence,
As we share our glorious days in this gift of Holy Alliance.

Dedicated to Rochester   J.G.K.
on the 7th anniversary of his adoption
June 23, 1993 in Rochester, NH
and anew on June 23, 2002

It Is Such a Secret Place

I know most people think of my feelings, and actions, for Maya
as being extreme. Maybe even "extreme" is an understatement.
—Martin Scot Kosins from *Maya's First Rose*

I HAVE WRITTEN THIS BOOK to honor a beloved little love, companion, friend, encourager, and angel with whom I have spent almost sixteen years. It is a journal of our love and blessed existence together and was begun immediately after Rochester went to Heaven. Without Rochester I did not know how to go on. We love each other so deeply I could not accept what had happened, and that I would not have him to hold in my arms any longer and to share life. I still have not accepted it. It washes over me and suffocates at times.

The day before he left I was shown by him a wondrous secret. The next evening as he left it was fulfilled in a deeply spiritual and other worldly manner. It has been my utter strength, even during all my ongoing grief and desolation. You will read about it in the pages of this journal. Too, writing this journal to honor him has sustained me when I thought I could not go on. I was to learn even more from him in these weeks and months that followed, for he is ever with me and I know he always shall be.

I have written this journal also to help myself while honoring Rochester. It is our journal. We belong to each other forever. I write this too to help others who may be grieving for a beloved animal companion or a human, for you see there is no difference in grieving. When you love deeply and unconditionally, and your beloved one has finished his life on earth, it can be devastating to lose his or her physical presence. As does

1

the author of the quotation that opens this Introduction, I believe that all life is sacred in every form and that the lives of people and animals are equal. It is not always accepted, even by those whom you consider close to you, but there are many in this world who believe in this way. There are less in the Christian tradition.

People wonder how you can be so devoted to an animal companion that you could give up people-oriented activities if it meant a too long absence from your animal. Many feel that it does not much matter if animals get sick or die, for you can always get another one. People wonder too, how the company of an animal companion for long hours each day can be fulfilling and satisfying. There are those who do find it so beautifully satisfying that an animal is their only companion day and night, and they will not give up that animal for another human. Only those who have lived with an animal in partial or total solitude can understand the beauty and depth of such a relationship; the sacredness, the commitment of both animal and human to the other, the unfathomable love, the extraordinary communication. Too, that when the relationship on earth is forced to end the human is left feeling like walking death, a shell, that does not think it possible to go on. And animals also feel this and grieve at the loss of their beloved human, sometimes refusing any sociability and food, and often die.

And not many want to be near such a person in this state, at least not alone with them for too long. Often family and friends space themselves from the one grieving and often they go for long periods at a time without contact, or forever. This grief is not understandable to most, and frequently not to your own family members.

Yet would they think you especially strange if you were grieving over a person? (Actually I was once reprimanded by a relative for having tears in her presence over my Dad, two months after his death.)

But there is no decision to be made by the one who has lost their blessed animal companion for they will never be the same, and if humans have distanced themselves or left completely it cannot be reasoned with. There is no desire to defend oneself. The one who experienced the loss will never change within. He would rather live with the precious memories and the spiritual presence of his animal companion than with those who were superficially his friends. The lack of understanding about the deaths of precious animal companions is the least of the pain and anguish felt. Frankly it really does not matter. The bereaved realizes this as time passes. What was never present in understanding when one's animal companion was alive cannot be expected to be different when one's beloved companion goes to Heaven. Expect nothing! Expect nothing— so as not to add to your heartbreak. Grieve for your beloved companion in your own way and do not expect others to understand. This can give a certain peace. And during your grief there may be one or two persons surface who truly are there if you need them.

Martin Scot Kosins, author of *Maya's First Rose*, whom I have quoted at the beginning of this Introduction tells in his book how certain friends faded away during his beloved dog Maya's last days and through this he learned who his truest friends were. He states:

> *What I will not understand as long as I live is why some people value the life of a person over the life of an animal. After all, is not life sacred in every form?*

He discusses how God knows when even a swallow falls and if God knows this with all else He cares about, then is not the life of the swallow as precious as his own?

But he wonders too why more people cannot understand that the life of a Dog who lived only for him was as sacred to Martin as the swallow is to God.

In moments when you have some clear thinking you will realize who believe in you no matter what and who was a great soul for you in your grief. You will always remember and appreciate that person or persons with all your heart and soul even if they are miles from you or you never see them again or you have never met face to face. Sometimes Angels enter your life when you are in utter despair. You will recognize them when they do. After all your animal companion too was and is your Angel. And too, who taught you to see beauty in the world, things you may never have noticed? It was your Angel companion, and so they attract other similar beings, and when one offers you understanding and solace you will recognize that the individual was sent by your beloved one.

And if some persons may have never known the blessed and true love of an animal, then they can not be expected to understand that your love for your companion could be of the greatest and highest dimension possible, and that your grief never leaves. It is impossible to explain. It is a bond totally different and unique from a love relationship with your dearest humans. Grief is a spiritual death while still alive.

Do not ever let anyone make you feel strange because you grieve.

I have been taught and have learned many things from Rochester in his *"School of Love,"* things I could not have learned elsewhere or from others. I am a far better person because of him, and I am so thankful and grateful for having been chosen by God to belong to Rochester. I always shall belong to him. In loving Rochester so deeply and indescribably I am expressing my gratitude continually.

Animal angels connect us to our higher nature because they love unconditionally, and they minister from their highest nature. They are messengers from God, and they exhibit spiritual qualities. Rochester demonstrated deep love, gratitude, concern, faithfulness, forgiveness, and forever gave of himself in continual companionship to me. He was not a mere mirror of me but made choices, remembered, and interpreted. Yes, and he used strategy and intelligence, and he was deeply compassionate. I lived continually with him and can attest to his precious qualities. He enriched my existence and I felt his deep spiritual protection, and indeed, I needed this when he came into my life and thereafter. When I looked into Rochester's golden eyes I knew he was an Angel. He is my Angel forever.

My husband Bob and I enjoy anagrams and one morning while in the depths of sadness Bob showed me a paper that just brought forth even more gratefulness. There in bold printing was the anagram for "ROCH-ESTER." The anagram was "HER ESCORT." How could this not be of God? It could not have been more true in our life here on earth together, and is proving to daily be true as Rochester's spirit accompanies me now. When he was here in all his physical handsomeness, he was truly *"my escort"* around this small cottage, and I felt his presence even when I had to be briefly away from him. This anagram and his title mean so much. I once wrote a poem about him called *"My Sella."* The word *"Sella"* means *"shadow"* So many tender memories. So many dear happenings and moments to think upon and record.

It is important for me at all times to have sacred space and an altar. I have written on this subject in two past books. Choose a sacred place in your home to be alone in your grieving. You may not always wish to be in this sacred space when you grieve, but it is essential to create one. I have needed such a place or places for years just in living, and now even more so. On your altar you can place pictures of your loved one, meaningful objects like rocks and stones (Rochester and I are fond of these), flowers, and other things that have significance that you two shared. Having an altar makes the surrounding area a sanctuary if you use it consistently. Some may light candles also.

For me, my beloved Rochester is symbolic of the Divine, an Angel in fur, and God -given breath of life bestowed on me at a time when I needed both an Angel and an enlivening prod to begin my life of writing. My Angel often laid upon my large desk that also held my altar that he inspired. He still lies there—beneath an icon of Christ. On August 13th in the period of writing this Introduction I dreamed again of Rochester. This time he was lying on his back and I was rubbing his soft white furred tummy as I did so often. He loved this, and he loved it in the dream too. Within the same week I had still yet another dream of him. He was standing still—his right side toward me in all his handsomeness on my desk.

His presence has always been a blessing on myself and my writing. A precious animal like Rochester with his love, warmth and affection, who loves to be near you and petted, is a Holy presence where God can meet you.

Aside from the altar on my desk I have one too on a wide wooden shelf at my kitchen window that contains treasures of nature, a small framed sketch of Christ, and a little kneeling figure of Mary, and a statue of St. Francis of Assisi. Also an African Violet, birds nests, and always pictures of Rochester. Recently I found an unusual piece of art work, a treasure to me on sale for under one dollar. It seemed to be created for me and I was in disbelief when I saw it. It is a standing archway of gray stone perhaps six inches high, with a door beneath the arch and dangling purple flowers and green leaves, Rochester's and my favorite colors above the door. A little path of rocks (we love rocks) leads upward to the door. I knew at once what it represented and felt God placed it there. You will understand as you read further in my journal why this simple object holds meaning and is now on this altar. It also has a small matching area of gray stone attached to it to hold a Rosary or candle or anything spiritual. For Rochester and me it is cradling a one decade green Irish Rosary.

Next to it stands a little 4x6-inch white tray I have had for years, given to me when I adopted Rochester. On it is a picture of an open window with flowers beneath the sill. A little cat sits on the sill, his back facing me. It speaks of Rochester on the window sill of Heaven to me now, looking out and waiting for my arrival, and to be with him for all eternity. When you grieve both old things and new suddenly take on significances they would not have had if you were not grieving.

In addition to these two altars I have had a prayer chair, a wooden adirondack chair upon a raised platform by our lake since we have lived here, and this too is sacred like an altar and where I pour myself out to God in grief now—and in many ways in past years. It is the place I could not wait to climb up into after my Dad's death in Pennsylvania and the long trip to New Hampshire that followed. I cried and cried as the lake breezes washed over me.

Creating an altar and sacred space is most important for your solace and grieving and prayers.

I write this now to say that the life and passing of an animal is important and worthy of recording, forever remembering, worthy of deep grieving. If you have a dear animal companion I would lovingly suggest that you begin to record his life and your life together in a journal. It is your treasure to do this and always have it. If your beloved animal is still with you try to begin now to write even if you never have before, and take many pictures. Some photos can go into your journals. If your beloved one has gone to Heaven in the past or in the present, a journal will help you in your grief. It will not take it away but you will feel like you are loving your dear one in still yet another way by recording his life that you treasured with all your heart. Your own written words and thoughts have a unique way of ministering to you. They are often like spiritual food for your soul.

Write about your life together and as you write you will cry, but your writing will be for all your life and you will value your journal with great appreciation and love. Only you can do this for your dear companion and yourself. On some other spiritual plane it will help you tremendously and honor your dear one. When you begin to write you will understand what I am saying.

I pray that this journal of Rochester's and mine will in some way help every reader no matter where they are in their lives at this time, for it is certain that though it may not yet have happened, one day you will have cause to deeply grieve. How I wish I could say this is not so. Take time to pray now so God can show you things—to connect with your animal. Please give dignity to your companion's passing.

While writing this Introduction I again saw Rochester in a vision here on the screened-in-porch where I have been writing on hot days. He looked at me and went under the green bench he loves so to nap as he did when I was writing here in times past. It was as natural in spirit as in days before in life. My heart pounded in joy. He is always here!

I share that beautiful vision and this wondrous thought with you as I close the Introduction, and as you begin to read this Journal.

What if you slept? And what if, in your sleep, you dreamed? And what if, in your dream, you went to heaven and there plucked a strange and beautiful flower? And what if, when you awoke, you had the flower in your hand? Ah, what then?

Written by one of the world's renowned poets, theologians and philosophers, Samuel Taylor Coleridge, this poem strikes my heart. It is an invitation to reconsider your thoughts about reality and to examine your imagination. It asks you to consider what you are capable of and what is possible in your dream state. This can apply to visions also. They are interconnected. I believe that with God all things are possible! What I have written on the pages of this Journal I believe expresses my heart and soul and deep beliefs, and that miracles occur, and that Rochester lives and is ever here. We have only to banish doubt, never waver, and believe. I do.

As you read please forgive me if I repeat anything, but this book is written in journal form and in journals one writes their innermost thoughts as they appear in their hearts and minds, and often the same thoughts repeatedly appear. It is through working through them in writing we are helped. I pray my journal that reveals my heart and soul and grief will in some way, some day, be a strength to you as other books

I have read ministered to me and continue to minister. Please, please, give dignity to your animal companion's passing. God bless you and all your dear animal companions.

This loving quotation by A.A. Milne is a metaphor for Rochester's and my life together. We too live in an Enchanted Forest and this "little girl" and her "cat" will always be playing.

So off they went together. But wherever they go and whatever happens to them on the way, in that enchanted place in the top of the Forest, a little boy and his Bear will always be playing.

PARADISE

I saw God in my precious cat
Gazing out through golden eyes—
I'd offer daily my fiat
I felt I lived in Paradise.

I was touched by love and grace
When I cupped his tiny face—
And kissed his forehead soft and dear
And wet his nose with my own tear.

For my dear   JGK
Rochester   July 17, 2002

We both just knew there was something extra in our lives each other. I can't imagine what it would be like without him. He is not only beautiful and kind, he is safe and reliable in a world that is often neither. He belongs to me, and yes, quite willingly, I belong to him. I feel sorry for people who can't relate to that. They have missed an awful lot.
              —Naturalist Roger Caras (Words written about his beloved dog),
                      President of the American Society for the Prevention
                                             of Cruelty to Animals

Tonight I will listen to the haunting music of *"The Fairy Ring."* You will understand why when you have come to the end of my journal.

Thank you.

BEYOND COMPREHENSION

Others saw him as a little cat—
　　O—He was so much more than that!
　　　He made the sun brighten—
　　　　the moon glow—
　　　　　the stars shine.
　　　　　　He was mine!

Constantly revealing
　　secrets of the universe—
　　　he brought healing,
　　　　love, joy, teaching—
　　　　　he was divine.
　　　　　　He was mine!

I was willingly reaching
　　to learn, explore, give more.
　　　He was the door
　　　　to another place—
　　　　　a world we shared.

Just gazing at his face
　　life was rearranged—
　　　I was changed.
　　　　We dared
　　　　　to live in another dimension.

We belonged to each other
　　in profound love.
　　　We were bound
　　　　yet it set us free.
　　　　　Our eternal bond
　　　　　　is beyond
　　　　　　　comprehension.

For Beloved Rochester　　　　　　　　　JGK
for June 23rd, 2002
16th Anniversary of his adoption

Holy Week

Life only demands from you the strength you possess.
—Dag Hammarskjold

March 3rd to 7th, 2002

CHESTER NEVER WAS A BIG EATEr yet he enjoyed his food. I had fun selecting food for him and pleasing him with his favorites. But the week of March 3rd things began to change and soon most seriously. On Sunday evening the third, he let his dinner sit after examining it. Monday he ate nothing all day although he jumped up on his table and checked out his dish. Tuesday was the same. I was beginning to feel a clong in my heart, a huge lump of worry. I prayed he would eat. I prayed for him continuously on normal days so I truly centered in on this concern this day. When he did not eat Sunday night I decided not to eat too, and began a fast of only liquids so that I could reinforce my prayers for him. I was still fasting by Tuesday night.

Tuesday evening without any food for energy, he caught a mouse. Leaping off of our banisterless living room stairs, he flew right over the chair sitting nearest these steps and across the living room to the front door, mouse in mouth. There, meeting him was Bob who opened the door so the two of them could go out on the screened-in porch. This was a routine well established and it went smoothly. Rochester paraded a bit to show off the mouse then as always dropped it, and while it was still stunned Bob placed a bowl over it. I praised Rochester for catching it as

10

I always do and he came indoors with me. Bob slipped a piece of cardboard under the bowl and carried the mouse off the porch and outdoors. Once released it took off into the winter night. All this took energy on Chester's part for he had also been briefly stalking the mouse previous to the catch. Never has he killed a mouse, only captured them so that we might release them. The chase did not seem to affect him physically.

By Wednesday I was so deeply concerned when he still refused to eat. I would open can after can each day to tempt him. This day I went into our small corner store and bought varieties he had never tasted before, varieties of fish. He had never had fish of any kind in his life for I had always followed the advice on feeding in the book *The Natural Cat* by Anitra Frazier, and it had proved to be a healthy way of eating. She had advised no fish for numerous reasons.

For the first time in three days Chester took a taste of food. Just a few little licks that he seemed to enjoy. But he stopped and my heart dropped. He never touched it again. I knew we had to take him to the Veterinarian which we did on Thursday at noon. We were told we would have to leave him over night for special feeding and to have an x-ray. Again, that clong in my heart for I did not want to part with him. We were always together! But we left him with much love and believing everything would be fine. I never allowed myself to think otherwise.

Once home after the 45 minute drive, the phone rang as we approached the door. We could not make it to the phone in time. It stopped ringing and began again once we were inside. Bob answered and was told the devastating news that Rochester had a large tumor on his liver and there was nothing that could be done to save him. Without ever having removed our jackets we turned and left the cottage and drove back to the office. There are no words to express what we were experiencing in the drive to Milton. I died before I got there.

Upon arrival we were told they would keep him and put him to sleep at once. I felt like I was suffocating!

I said "no!" This horrendous news had been thrust upon us without warning, but an inner energy or power came over me and I said "no" again. Because he and I communicate, I knew he was in no pain nor had he been all week. We needed time to say good-bye and time alone and only then could I think of the unthinkable. They gave us til noon the next day but I wanted the latest time they could give—which was 2:45 PM. It still was not long enough. When we got home Bob called for the latest appointment and we were given 5 PM.

The drive home had been unbearable but Chester laid in his carrier that was on my lap and we held hands just as we had earlier on the way down. In all the thousands of miles he had travelled from Pennsylvania to New Hampshire and back in his first ten years of life 'til we moved to New Hampshire permanently, he had always thrown up at the beginning and end of every trip of the 420 miles. On this 45 minute trip to and from the Veterinarian's he did not, nor did he the next day. He just laid quietly holding my hand or laying his head on my hand. He was too sick to be sick. My little beloved just lay there.

His story of his last day home with us needs to be told separately and too, all that followed—for it truly is Holy. Like Christ, Chester lived out his last hours on a Friday, a Friday three weeks before Good Friday and Holy Week. Rochester experienced his own Holy Week as did we with him, and his own Holy Friday. I will never forget it all until the day I join him in Heaven.

But first—let me tell you more about our life together, a life that he made rich with love and joy. I shall begin on the day after he entered heaven.

My Angel

Do you know what you are?
You are a marvel. You are unique.
In all the years that have passed,
there has never been another ... like you.

—Pablo Casals (1878–1973)

Musings on Mourning
written randomly over the week of
March 10th to 17th, 2002

*M*ANY FEEL THE ULTIMATE RELATIONSHIP is with a human, or that perhaps even a situation in life can bring total happiness and fulfillment. And then there are those who have realized that companionship and selfless love shared with an animal companion has been a fulfilling and ultimate joy separate from all other relationships. This joy can come into our lives when we are in desperate need and be an intervening Angel. Rochester was and is that Angel to me.

When Chester (yes, someone who is greatly and deeply loved is called by many names) came into my life, life was not good or fun or being happily lived. Life was extremely serious. He brought sunshine to the clouds of sadness both through his spiritual presence and literally by his precious orange marmalade fur that was truly like the Autumn sunsets on our lake. His white fur spoke of his purity and innocence so fresh from

13

God. Yes, an Angel had moved in with us and I loved him beyond words. Even In my own journals I can not find adequate words to describe the depth of my love for Rochester.

Often when you love to the heights and depths and so extraordinarily, there is no factual reasoning to your thinking. You just believe implicitly as I did in a non-arguable fact, and refuse to be shaken even by your very own fleeting negative thought that might arise in a moment when you are in despair and think all is falling down around you. I loved with the absolute belief, as our days together in happiness and joy passed, that Rochester would never die! I believed we would never be physically separated! I live in the ether—not in objective reality. He was like a dream and from another realm. He never even aged! Angels do not age! Each dawn breaks as does my heart, but a day is not big enough to hold all my tears, and they spill over into the next day and the next and the next. Each hour and minute filled with memories so exquisitely cherished is re-examined and re-lived, and kissed and caressed in spirit as I did to him in reality in the years we shared life moment by moment.

I collected those moments in my heart each like a priceless pearl given by God. They will sustain and nourish until we are together again for all eternity.

The unthinkable has come true. Rochester's physical presence is absent yet felt as keenly and lovingly and intensely as if he can be seen. He is here! And I still live my hours and days in his gracious and gently electrifying presence. It shall always be so for I am open to all that he has to teach me in our new dimension of living, just as I have been since the day we first began our life together.

Because of our ongoing and eternal bond and connection, I am experiencing the passage of time in a new reality. The word *"closure"* that I have heard lovingly spoken to me several times, a goal that perhaps is achievable and obtainable for some, is not in my vocabulary nor is it desired. I have lived through the deaths of human loved ones and they are ever with me. Tears for them are continual and surface upon deliberate meditation on them, or when their images and connected memories surface unexpectedly. I would not want it any other way. Each dream of them, each rediscovered journal entry, or fleeting image in the mind's eye is significant and cherished. I have written about them in my books as well as my journals for they continue to live in another dimension just beyond a veil and are very much a part of my spiritual life. Never would I want closure. It does not matter that their physical absence still brings tears. They are worth it. And my beloved Rochester is surely worthy of my grieving and every tear that spills from my eyes, for he is a precious miracle from God that gave me new life, and courage, and changed me forever for the better. He is my little beloved.

I want no relief from the tears for that is not living. I want our new form of life to be alive and filled with surprises and overflowing with the enchantment we shared in our former life, and eternal love so intense that there is never relief, just the realization that this is perhaps like being in a vestibule. Eventually there is more, and more, and more, when we are once again physically together—only this time it will be for all eternity in the vastness of Heaven never again to be physically separated.

Closure is a strange word to me for why would I want any type of finality to a life lived with someone I cherish? Instead I want the door from this life and the one to eternity (one and the same) to be ever open, or perhaps not exist at all! I envision a vastness of beauty (the ether?) where the possibility for meetings and visions and communication exist. I believe in visits from our loved ones unexpected, unexplainable, anywhere, and too, in dreams. If I close my mind and keep compartments for those who have gone before me and for myself, I close off the possibilities also of any significant interchange because I will live without expectation. If I refuse to follow a rule, be it assumed, religious, or unthinkable, and ask God to surprise me, I will then expect to experience Rochester every day of my life here on earth in multitudinous forms until we are together forever once more.

Each one experiences grief in a different way and grief is on-going. Closure indicates an ending, a completion. I could not bear that! Rochester was and is essential to my life! He is the only one I ever spent a solitary life style with for just short of sixteen years, together daily! Yes, of course there were others who would occasionally appear, especially my Bob, but only rarely for short segments during the day. But Bob, Chester and I were together each night. And earlier I reared six children, but I was not with them all day each day or even every night. They had their activities as well as their home life and their respected privacy. My days were spent writing these past sixteen years in the company of a precious little being whom I loved fiercely, honored always, and respected in the highest manner possible. He also loved, honored, and respected me in ways so endearing I was often in tears because of his greatness of love and the ways in which he expressed it. Besides verbally and in great affection physically, I wrote about him in my books and composed endless poetry in tribute to him, and enhanced my journal pages with our life together.

I shall always celebrate Rochester—telling stories, sharing memories, and writing, for it is my way to stay sane and keep his being alive, and for me to survive.

I believe, like that possible door I mentioned earlier, that instead of the door, our grief itself becomes the passage way or opening that connects us forevermore to our loved ones. Therefore it becomes Holy for it is a divine connection or link, never shut off. We live it continually and it is absorbed into souls, into our hearts, and it is a necessary part of living. That is my grieving. Though we hope and pray we may never have to go through it, grieving is inevitable for if we have lived in the company of one (or more) that we have deeply loved, unless we are taken first, we will also deeply grieve.

No one can tell us how to grieve or for how long. Every one is different therefore each will grieve in different ways. When we die our grief will end and we will be reunited forever with those for whom we grieved. Perhaps then in our ecstatic eternal joy of reunion someone or ones on earth will begin a new cycle of grieving—this time for us.

September 8, 2002

UPON COMPLETING THIS ENTIRE JOURNAL I discovered in my reading a poem by the great poet Rumi—a man from another time and place. It was as if a portion of the poem was written for Rochester and me, and that he knew what we are experiencing in our life together day by day, and that this poem was intended to be placed after this Journal entry in March. For you see though I write this now and leave this poem upon the page, it seems like it is always in the present and that I am placing it here the same day I completed this Journal entry in March, six months previous. Rochester and I are truly living exactly as I have written about throughout this Journal, in the present and eternal moment of when it all began. It is a gift, an eternal blessing, and it can be yours also.

You must ask for what you really want.
Don't go back to sleep.
People are going back and forth
Across the doors where the two worlds touch.
The door is round and open.
Don't go back to sleep.

—Rumi

Come with me now to where our sadness first began—to the entrance to our *Passage Through Grief*.

A Circle of
Eternal Love

St. Francis etched in finest pewter
On the round tag at his neck
Does bedeck—and yes, protect—
The life of my dear feline suitor.

A red heart, too, has name and number—
Symbolic of the Sacred Heart—
And when in play or deepest slumber —
God's with my precious counterpart.

Saturday, March 9, 2002

I LEFT MY BELOVED ROCHESTER with a woman I did not know and came home instead with only his collar. I slipped it on my arm under my sweater to keep it safe on that drive home that I do not remember. I could not see on the drive home.

At home the little pewter St. Francis medal and red metal heart with his veterinarian information on jangled each time I moved my arm. There is a tiny bell on it too. They are attached to the new purple nylon collar we had put on him only five weeks or so ago. He looked so handsome in it, but looked even more handsome with no collar, as he does on the cover of my book, *Compassion for All Creatures*. He is so beautiful on the cover of that book. When I would walk in Bookland, my favorite bookstore in Sanford, Maine and see copies of this book dis-

18

played in various places, my heart would melt. To think that my little beloved was there for all to see. So many commented on the beauty of that cover there. His eyes look right at me. I used to stand and stare in their store window where many copies of *Compassion* appeared for many weeks displayed beautifully by my friend Cheryl who worked in Bookland, a friend I had come to know by shopping there and through my books. To think that my precious Rochester was in this store window (and other windows elsewhere) made me feel such gratitude and love for him. It was *his* book. All my books are his.

This day after his leaving I get out his previous collar from my drawer. I have each one he has ever worn. Though he remained indoors for his safety's sake, he still wore a collar on the chance he ever slipped out. But he did not try to do that. His previous collar is red and soft. I had carefully printed his name and phone number on it but it had almost worn off, though can still be read. He had worn this soft collar for several years and it looked attractive against the white fur at his neck. It too had had the same St. Francis medal upon it and red heart, until we transferred them to the purple collar. I held it in my hand crying and then kissed it. I removed the purple collar slipping it over my hand, not unhooking it. Saying a prayer for my little Chester I slipped the red one over my left hand and onto my wrist. It was loose but could not fall off. I wanted it to remain hooked in the same hole on the collar as it had been when around Rochester, just as the purple one shall remain hooked. Forever hooked, it was a never ending circle symbolizing eternal love—the love Rochester and I share. This was the collar I would wear, the red one—not the newer one. This is the one he had worn much longer and he had it on in so many, many pictures I had taken of him.

Though I have worn other things for him through the years, a little silver cat head necklace given to me the year Chester came into my life and never removed since, a silver ring with an amethyst heart symbolizing our love, and a silver ring bearing an image of a sitting cat, this red collar was now going to be mine forever.

My left arm will indeed hold significance. On that wrist also is a silver cuff bracelet similar to those worn by many for those missing in action in Viet Nam. I began to wear this bracelet in January, obtaining it after I learned such bracelets were available for the victims of September 11th on CNN. Though names are available of Firemen, Policemen, the victims at the Pentagon and from the field in Pennsylvania where the plane crashed, I requested a name of someone who died in the World Trade Center since that is where I saw the first planes enter that horrendous morning. My bracelet has a fine man's name on (a husband, father and grandfather), who died in The World Trade Center in the offices of Cantor-Fitzgerald. The bracelet is called a Mercy B.A.N.D. and is to be worn forever. The initials stand for *"Bearing Another's Name Daily."*

And so I add another band—red, next to the silver, and I too shall *"bear Rochester's name daily."* And when the name wears off perhaps I shall add it again. I will know what to do when the time comes. And I will wear it until he and I are reunited in Heaven.

His little tinkling tags that dangle—
Let me know that he is near.
His dear approach from any angle—
One cannot help but overhear.

Ah—now he springs onto my lap—
He cares not its the thirtieth of May—
He snuggles down into his nap—
I hold his paw
and still in awe
I celebrate his sixth birthday.

(Poem: Rochester's birthday)

Dedicated to   JGK
Rochester Harry Whittier Kolb
on his birthday—

—and now in these sad, sad days.

Our Memorial Service

The days are few from our mortal birth—
that we walk with God on His sweet green earth.
But in corridors of eternal time—
joy with Him will be sublime.

—Bob Kolb

Sunday, March 10, 2002

HE GRIEF IS SO OVERWHELMING AND INTENSE I elect to stay home from Church, and Bob agrees. I do not want to leave our cottage and woods or meet people. I cannot pretend normalcy and smiles. Quiet and aloneness is necessary.

We instead have a loving Memorial Service for Rochester here in the living room where we three were together in the evenings and Sunday afternoons, a room he loves, and with sliding glass doors through which he watches the birds and squirrels.

We select the most obvious and appropriate hymn and meditation from our own book we wrote, *Whispered Notes*. Rochester has heard the hymns played on the piano and the meditations read aloud throughout his life. The ones we select are titled "A Place in Eternity." You, as reader, can read the words of the hymn that I include and be part of our private little service for Rochester, by turning to the hymn in the back of this book. Though the words are inspiring they bury me in sadness and grief. I am crushed and despairing, and long for him to return.

21

When my work here has ended—
I'll at last be there too.
For His promise to join Him in the church triumphant
I know to be true.

—Bob Kolb

One day I will be with Chester again for all eternity.

In Remembrance

Where belief is painful, we are slow to believe.

—Ovid

Monday, March 11, 2002

I FEEL AS IF I AM BEHIND A VEIL OR SHEER CURTAIN looking at everything from another world. Nothing seems real. Perhaps when perceptions are distorted and I am in disbelief it is a form of protection. I feel detached and yet intense. The emptiness of this small cottage without his physical presence is painfully evident, and I cry again and again.

All weekend in my pain of remembering, loss, and incredible sorrow, I know I have to acknowledge my little one's passing in my latest book. We know it is going to press at any moment, and so Bob writes up a loving passage about Rochester and e-mails it. He asks my publisher, Paul Clemens, to put one of Rochester's pictures with it that he has, and to place it in the back of the book. I can hardly believe what we are doing.

It is then I decide to further honor our little beloved and family member and his precious life by sending out loving announcements of his entrance into Heaven. Bob and I both write a memorial containing words expressing all that he means to us. We combine into one all from the two that tells of his beauty, devotion, life, and mission. It is a longer memorial for this announcement being mailed, and for this journal, than for my book now going to press. It speaks my heart. I ask Bob to make many

23

prints in green ink on 8.5 x 11 white paper, for had I written them by hand they would have been written in green ink with a brand of pen I have used since 1989 when we became vegetarians for the sake of the animals and Rochester. The green ink speaks of the natural world to me, and our woods and life shared with Rochester.

Above the message that honors him is a handsome picture of him, his beautiful golden eyes looking into my soul. I immediately begin to address envelopes (in green ink also) though I will not finish them all today. I am certain it will take me several days to finish. Writing is a part of our entire life together and it is a most loving act to do to honor Chester right now. He is with me as I write. He is always with me when I write. He is always with me forever.

I need others to look upon his countenance and remember him too, whether they have met him before or not. Some only know him through my writing and books. I need to pause and tell the world about my beloved little feline companion.

Over the weekend, the two days that followed Holy Day, I began making notes about the book I will write about Rochester. I will put aside the present book he and I have been working on since late fall of 2001, and begin this new book, one to honor his precious life and our years spent together. The book you are reading now.

It is the only way I can get through these days without his physical presence. I will keep him vitally alive, for he is through my writing, for writing is prayer to me. Writing will keep him alive and keep me sane. Everything I am doing is surreal. It cannot possibly be me doing these things. Why Chester is asleep up in his quilt there in our writing room! I just cannot see him through my endless tears. I touch my swollen lips that remain from Friday evening, and reality pulls me down into despair. I cannot write of the cause of their swolleness now, but I am humbled by it.

The page that follows is a copy of the memorial we sent out in Chester's memory. The picture was in color on the memorial. The red band around his neck is the one now upon my left arm forever, minus his two tags.

Rochester, beloved feline companion, confidant, counselor,
and ministering angel, finished his work here
after almost 16 years (minus one month) and passed on.
He was a motivator and enabler to me and
unselfishly gave of himself in deep love continually.
He was with me every day—all day while I wrote—
since he was eight weeks old and was my inspiration.
He was with me through every night.
Rochester was the Star of every book I wrote.
He was a most loving friend to Bob.
His sudden illness, diagnosed only Thursday, March 7th,
brought about his reluctant departure.
We were with him 'til he passed—and after.
He shall forever be with me in soul and spirit,
to help and inspire until we are together once more.

Rochester entered Heaven
March 8, 2002
5:07 PM

WRITE

When your heart is breaking—
  and your soul despairing—
    and you're crying out in pain—

Your pen is aching—
  and oh so caring—
    the very gift to keep you sane!

Write!

For Rochester   JGK
My companion in writing.   March 11, 2002

In the Beginning

God never loved me in so sweet a way before. Tis He alone who can such blessings send. And when His love would new expressions find, He brought thee to me and He said—Behold a friend.

—Unknown

Tuesday, March 12, 2002

I CANNOT NOW EVER IMAGINE my life without Rochester. Rochester is named for the town in which I received him and adopted him—and I felt it might possibly be the town in which he was born. He is also known affectionately by the shortened version of his name—"*Chester.*" Bob alone calls him *Harry*, a secret name of acceptance when Rochester first came into our lives. Bob had never known or had a cat before and was reluctant to let my daughter Janna and me adopt him. Not able to express it, my husband had given our little cat another name, his secret way, perhaps even surprising and inexplicable to himself, of showing affection for this tiny kitten. Yet when I had suggested Rochester for a name on our drive home that day after adopting him, although it was accepted by the three of us, Bob also added "Call him Chester for short." But he remained "*Harry*" to Bob always, but forever Rochester or Chester to me. Everyone knew him by Rochester or Chester.

On June 23, 1986 God placed a gift down for me on a bench in a small mall in Rochester, New Hampshire and I did not know this gift was to be bestowed on me. Words still cannot convey the depth of the joy that this gift has brought into my life.

27

His gift of love that warm June morning took the form of a tiny marmalade and white furry kitten approximately eight weeks old, and my life was changed forever in receiving that precious gift.

And so—life was different. A beautiful creature of God lives with me, sleeps with me, and spends the majority of his hours near me or on my lap, only now he does so in spirit—and my life is enriched because of him. I see with new spiritual eyes matters I did not see vividly and with my whole heart before he came to love me. He has changed my husband's life too. I have written in great detail about the ways in which Rochester affected our lives in all of my previous books. He is an Angel and his presence changed us—and continues to do so.

Because of Rochester and the great love we share, I became a vegetarian for his sake and the sake of all animals in September 1989. My husband did also shortly after. Because of Chester and turning to reading to learn more, I learned the word *Ahimsa*. This means *"harmlessness"* or not hurting, and that is a Sanskrit word for compassion. Wherever *Ahimsa* is found, there is deep compassion, unselfishness, and service to others, and a refraining from causing pain and suffering to any living creature. It naturally implies non-killing. In the numerous books in which I came upon the true meaning of this word, I also learned in each that to not cause injury truly means total abstinence from causing ANY harm or pain whatsoever to ANY living creature, either by thought, word, or deed. It is LOVE! Universal Love! In the long ago it was said that Ahimsa was prescribed by very wise men to eliminate cruel and brutal tendencies in man.

Ahimsa is said to be the highest and noblest of traits. To sum up all that *Ahimsa* is, is to learn that *Ahimsa* or non-violence has proven to be a great and mighty Spiritual force.

Rochester's presence and love in my life brought all of this light to my soul and caused me also to investigate and then to write down all that I was shown and all the personal joys I have been experiencing since sharing my life with my beloved Chester. We write and write and love and love and that shall not stop now. Our love is eternal and we are very present to each other, and he shall forever influence my life for good as he has done since we first met and belonged to each other.

TAKEN

In the living of my life
        my Rochester always took part—
O it was like a knife
        thrust into my heart—
            when he was taken.

I did not want to waken—
        not see his little face,
There in his place
        upon me in sleep.

I just weep—and weep and weep.

For dear Rochester   JGK
                                      March 12,2002

A Ritual of Bonding

We do not need words
Our eyes speak—
Our touch reveals
Each new day we discover new beauty
In silence
Of each other.

—Walter Rinder

Thursday, March 14, 2002

AFTER ROCHESTER CAME INTO OUR LIVES he was gently showing me secrets in the course of each day. He selected an evening when the two of us were all alone, to teach me about *"bonding."* Three days after he came to live with us, everyone had gone to bed, and as I sat on the sofa in our small cottage on Lake Balch, my little Rochester slept beside me, curled up tightly. Soon he wakened and stretched his tiny little body and looked directly into my eyes. That alone struck my soul, this meeting of our eyes in the silence of the room.

Suddenly he came over onto my lap and sat there momentarily, continuing to look at me. I was so moved by his beauty and felt his closeness in a new way. Then something almost mysterious took place, and I have never forgotten it, nor the feeling that it enkindled within me. Often when I think back on it, I have tears and am *"held"* in a strange way as I reflect on it.

30

Since writing these words some years ago in a journal and then in a book *(Compassion for All Creatures),* I did not know then that I would continue to have other mysterious and precious incredible moments and exchanges throughout our life together. They are all recorded in other journals and published books.

But on this particular night I am telling you about this tiny creature literally walked up the front of me and, with his tiny face just opposite mine, bumped his small forehead to the front of mine, several times. Then he climbed onto my right shoulder and went behind my neck, partially on me and partially on the sofa back. He began to play with my small gold hoop earrings, and I felt his paws on my head as he nestled his face into the back of my hair. Then he appeared on my left shoulder, rubbing into the side of my cheek. Down he went onto the front of my shirt, and then turned around and again to face me. Again he came up face to face with me, and again he bumped his little forehead into mine several more times. No sound was made, simply the meeting of our heads and minds.

Again he went onto my right shoulder and repeated all he had done before, playing with my earrings and hair. Again he appeared on my left shoulder. Once more he went through all he had done the first two times, the bumping of our heads and the nestling behind my head to play with earrings and hair, then down to my lap. When his eyes met mine this time, I knew in my heart that a most significant event had just transpired. It had almost been a little ritual, this exact repeat, three times, of bumping his head to mine, and then little displays of affection as he made his way behind my neck to circle around again.

This was something mystical to me. It was not an ordinary happening. Something deep within myself assured me that Rochester and I were bonded in a most unique way. I would go over and over it in my mind, that such a tiny little one repeated such a loving act three times and had communicated to me through this act and the love in his eyes that he had "*somehow*" made me "*his.*" It was not until several weeks later, upon reading a wonderful book about cats, that I learned that "*head bumping*" is indeed a treasured happening between cat and human. It is the cat's way of telling his loved one that they belong to each other, that the human is the "*cat's*" person. But actually, it is more so that the cat owns the person, and from that moment on a faithfulness remains. Certainly, in our relationship Rochester and I have been eternally bonded and a most loving and spiritual relationship exists. He is mine and I am his, and he never minded that all in his small world were informed of this.

Without my knowing that such a bonding is given by a cat when he has chosen his human, my tiny Rochester had made known to me, through his loving ritual and eyes that held me fast, that something on another plane was indeed taking place. He had even chosen a time of silence, when we were totally alone, for this marriage of hearts between kitten and human.

I am owned by a little cat!

Later we would learn to spiritually communicate with each other in still yet a different dimension. Our deep love was such that we continually tried to express this gift of our love daily as we spent our lives together.   In 1991 I wrote a very long poem, and one verse of it now seems right to close these remembrances.

BONDED

Into my life Rochester came
And I have never been the same.
We are bonded—of one heart.
In all I do he is a part.
He travels with us everywhere
And helps me write by being there.
We're vegetarians—He did that!
Precious white and marmalade cat.

The First Friday

What greater gift than the love of my cat?
—Charles Dickens

Friday, March 15, 2002

THIS FRIDAY WITHOUT ROCHESTER'S PHYSICAL PRESENCE, and last Friday's occurrences, are such an anomaly that I cannot bear to write personal thoughts of it all. They are ripping my mind apart and that is enough!

Instead, I am replacing these wounding and horrendous thoughts with a poem I wrote for him with such love many years ago. I have always appreciated Dickens quote and used it, and the poem also, in a recent book Rochester and I wrote together, *Journal of Love*. I am stealing the quote and poem from my own book, for my present mind is crippled in grief. Such happy days writing that book and the writing of the poem. Rochester symbolizes love and joy, then, now, and forever. And I am still holding him, and ever shall.

33

OWNED BY MY CAT*

Right now—

I am sitting here holding my little cat—
And there is nothing—no nothing—as important as that.
I have put down my paper and put down my book,
To make room for his person—so I can just look—
At him curled in my arm asleep purring loudly
And I feel so honored and embrace him so proudly—
For I am sitting here holding my little cat—
And there is nothing—no nothing—as important as that.

For dear little   JGK
Rochester   October 15, 1993
                                         New Hampshire

I am sitting here holding my little cat, early 1987

Seeking Help

*Once death touches our lives we feel changed by it, we are less likely
to want to gather up the energy it takes to slip out the door.
We don't want to leave the safety of our surroundings.*
—Carol Staudacher, *A Time to Grieve*

Monday, March 18, 2002

I HAVE REMAINED INSIDE OUR COTTAGE or outdoors near the lake for
nine days. Grieving, writing, staring into space, and being with Bob
in the evenings and occasionally during the days is all I can do. I am
consumed by grief, and the emptiness of the cottage without Rochester's
physical presence. But his spirit is wherever I am. He is here every
moment.

I do not go to the Post Office or the grocery store, and Bob does not
mind picking up the mail each afternoon. We do not attend church for
two Sundays. Instead we have our own worship services together reading
meditations and hymns from our own book, *Whispered Notes*, that we
authored together years before Rochester was born. We dedicate our
times of worship together to him. And we pray together. I simply cannot
leave our property and venture out of these woods for fear of having to
talk to someone we know. I need the safety of our world, the peacefulness
of the woods and lake and singing birds, and too , the ever underlying
silence. I need to be with Rochester in this new dimension of living and

find my way in our new existence. I am no longer fasting but I have no appetite and eat little.

We decide today—on this Monday—it is time I leave the woods. The destination chosen is the Walden Book Store in Rochester, twenty-five miles away. It is the town in which I adopted my beloved little Rochester so many years ago (oh they went too quickly!) and of whose name I gave him (mentioned in a previous meditation). And it was also to this town and to this bookstore I first came before making a week long retreat alone with Rochester three months after he came into my life. We had come from Pennsylvania for this retreat. Just seeing his name on so many road signs as we drive south down Route 16 overwhelms me, but his name is everywhere in our area. These signs will be a constant memorial to him in our minds and hearts, and will always remain.

Ever since Rochester came to us I would say prayers of gratitude for him in our lives whenever we drove through or past the town of Rochester or anywhere near the spot where we adopted him. I always will do this as I do this day.

We arrive at the Lilac Mall (Lilacs are New Hampshire's state flower) and Bob goes off to do errands and I go into Waldens. I spend the next two hours there in a daze and silence and having only to speak to the saleswoman when I check out. I roam and browse and cry and eventually have four books in my hands all on grieving. There are no books that speak about grieving over our precious animal companions. I will have to reread the chapter of the subject of grieving in my own book with Rochester's beautiful face on the cover, and keep writing this very book I started this past week to help myself and others too. Never did I think I would be reading my own book or even writing that particular chapter—in regard to Rochester. But I need to read about grief because I am submerged in it. I need to read about grief in regard to losing a beloved companion and these books I have chosen regarding human loss are appropriate for my grief regarding Rochester. When you love, grief is grief. Although I have written a very happy book (*Beneath the Stars and Trees*), a joyful and peaceful book, in response to grieving I experienced several years ago, that was a different type of sorrow. It was in response to a situation that caused great pain, and so writing about all that I experience living in nature in the woods with Rochester and Bob, was my gift to myself and healing therapy for dealing with that sorrow. It was a situation not to be compared in any way whatsoever to Rochester's passing. Rochester's is a grief and passing so sacred it has no comparison ever.

I did not read books on grieving back when I wrote that book in late 1999 and spring and summer of 2000. I had Rochester's physical presence always then, so comforting. Writing was my total therapy—and prayer, for writing is prayer to me too. But I do need books to read about grieving in regard to Chester and so I buy four. I also buy a beautiful journal to use just to write in about Chester; his life, his passing, and my continued new life with him in presence. I will put his messages to me in it just as I kept a journal with all his messages in before he passed away. Many of these are in his book and mine, *Journal of Love*, about communicating with animals through writing. I will record all that happened since March 8th that up 'til now I was recording in the faithful steno pad I always carry with me. I knew soon I would buy a special journal for these sacred memories and his life.

The new journal I find is so perfect. The night sky here in New Hampshire is always so brilliant with stars and the moon in all its forms, and it is a magical and spiritual part of living here. It was part of my life with Chester. I wrote poems for him comparing him to the stars and angels. He is both of these in my life forever.

This new journal has two half moons facing each other and touching at their points forming a whole, which speaks of an eternal circle to me and Rochester's and my forever and unbroken eternal love. The journal is even titled *"Forever"* above the moon, which confirms that it is meant for Rochester and my entries about him, and our life together. Stars twinkle on a darkened sky behind the moon, and the sky is deep shades of night blue and red. The cover is a light tan, and the trim on the journal is red, a symbol of the one heart we share. It has a red elastic strap to slip over the cover to keep it closed. It is the perfect journal for sacred notes, poems, and his life. He is in all of my own personal journals and written about again and again—but this is his journal for past, present, and future—and I will get another just like it if I soon fill the pages as I do with my own journals. I envision many volumes of journals filled for him or surely for as long as I live.

This has been a most meaningful day and has filled me with resolve in various ways all in regard to my little one, my little eternal companion, Rochester.

Arriving home is the hardest moment of all, for it is only the second time I arrive and not hear my little guy walking across the piano keys to wait for us by the front door. The silence of it all makes me feel broken and weak.

And always after we opened the door he would run briefly onto the porch to greet us, then dash into the bedroom to await me. I would go directly there and we would sit on the side of the bed together while he too walked on my lap and rolled around next to me wanting to be patted, and he would bump his head into mine. I would let our little ceremony of welcome continue until he ended it, then we would go out into the living room. I go into the bedroom today too, for I know he is with me, beside me, and on my lap. I will always go into the bedroom to greet him when I arrive home.

In a few hours I begin reading my first new book on grieving. I say a prayer that this one, and the others, will be supportive in ways I cannot quite yet understand, for I have only begun to know this grief. It is almost like an entity that is always there. Rochester is helping me too. He always has been my little teacher and Angel.

Rochester always loved books, 1987

EVER-SHINING STAR

The years go by
        and you and I—
Commune and talk
        and walk our walk—
                together—
        and with God.

Golden time as one—
        sunsets when day is done.
Hours filled with writing
        and you—my soul—highlighting
                all—
        with each gentle nod.

What priceless gift you are!
My ever-shining star.
Rochester.

Written for Rochester   JGK
My Star   Jan 15, 1999

Rochester on retreat with me, September 1986

Home Again

*Hope begins in the dark, the stubborn hope that if you just show up
and try to do the right thing, the dawn will come.
You wait and watch and work: you don't give up.*

—Anne Lamott

Wednesday, March 20, 2002

A CALL COMES IN THE MORNING and it is the Veterinarian's office telling us Rochester's ashes are there and may be picked up. I have been waiting for this call day after day. Fear would come over me that something might go wrong and I would not get him back. We stop what we are doing to drive there immediately. Once there, Bob thoughtfully parks the car in the lot so it faces away from the office. I do not allow my eyes to look in any rear view mirrors. My heart is pounding. He is carrying a gift for the doctors there, two copies of my books, the two that have on the covers handsome pictures of Rochester. These books are so they will remember, at least for awhile, that an extraordinary little marmalade and white cat named Rochester Harry Whittier Kolb passed through their establishment—and that he really is very special. He is an author and Angel.

In exchange Bob returns only minutes later with a white plastic bag containing a lovely floral tin receptacle, that is 5 by 3.5 inches, that is securely holding and protecting Rochester's ashes. It is such a relief to have this box in my hands and on my lap. We drive home almost in total silence. I cannot believe what my hands are embracing. Without his ashes I would be crazy, and with them I am crazy too. It must all be a very, very bad dream. When we drive down our hill and park next to our cottage we will hear Rochester walking across the piano keys to wait by the door to greet us. But there is silence and I continue crying.

At home we carefully lift out the tin and treat it delicately. I sit it on the sofa where he always enjoys being with me. We do not look inside the tin. The lid is taped shut. The ashes must be contained in a wrap of some sort for they shift in the can when moved, seeming encased. This tin will be my silent companion forever. I hold it too, and hug it to me and kiss it, and cry and cry. Bob sits silently with me.

There are papers in the bag with the tin telling of other fine containers and receptacles that can be bought for the ashes to replace the tin. There is a dignified certificate in an envelope addressed to us from Angel View Cemetery and Crematorium in South Middleboro, Massachusetts. This is near the Rhode Island border. My little one's body has been far from me in this past week and a half but now is safely back in the home he loves and with his loved ones. Still yet another new kind of existence is about to begin. How am I existing at all? I really do not know.

Precious Memorial

Open the door of your heart to the voice of an Angel

—Unknown

Friday, March 22, 2002

DAILY I OPEN MY HEART TO ROCHESTER. Today we place Rochester's memorial of words paying tribute to his life with photograph above them, in a dark green frame. This is the memorial we sent out to family and friends the first week of his physical absence. I take a picture of it on the wall after we hang it in the living room next to Bob's recliner, and opposite the sofa where Chester and I sit each night a few feet across the room next to the sliding doors. I also place an identical memorial in green frame in my writing room.

I cannot bear Fridays and their memories. I place instead on this page a poem of the past to honor my beloved little Angel.

42

HOLY GUISE

In your presence
       is wisdom, truth
          and beauty.
I see the face of God.
The slightest nod
       and gentle blinking
          of your golden eyes—
Is a sacred linking,
       revealing anew
       your Holy guise.
It is no surprise
       to realize
          you are an Angel—
That my depleted soul
       needed to be whole.
Yet daily I am in awe—
       as I enclose your soft white paw
          into my hand.
I shall never understand
       why I was chosen.

In deepest gratitude
to God for Rochester—
for his birthday.
(estimated birth—April 15
celebrated May 30)

JGK
May 18, 1998

Presents of Presence

We are not human beings on a spiritual path,
but spiritual beings on a human path.

—Jean Shimoda Bolen

Monday, March 25, 2002
Today I am given a miracle!

EARLY IN THE MORNING our bedroom door was always opened and Rochester would eventually leave and wait in the living room for me to get up. Occasionally he would come back to walk on top of me or settle down again but both were to motivate me to come into the other room. Most mornings however, he would wait in the living room on a favorite spot on the green rug, or watch the birds on the deck through the sliding glass doors. Once I joined him, and Bob also, we had breakfast together and began our day. Bob would go to his office a few yards from our cottage and Rochester and I would go upstairs to our writing room to spend the day together while I wrote. Our little heaven.

On this Monday morning of March 25th I wake in tears upon the realization of Rochester's permanent physical absence. Each morning since March 8th I am devastated in this way. I wipe my eyes and try to calm myself, and look out into the hall as I have been accustomed to do for so many years. Standing in the hall is my beloved Rochester! The left side of his sweet body is facing me and his head is turned toward me just looking in at me with his golden eyes—a scene I have seen so often in the

44

past. He is real and alive and waiting for me! I am not delusional! It is as in reality! I am not asleep nor in any semi sleep. It is not a dream! It lasts only a couple of seconds, this precious image or vision, and then he is gone. I continue to stare in wonder, tears streaming down my face anew. He has appeared to me! Instantly I know in my spirit he is comforting me, assuring me he is always with me.

When I go to our writing room soon after I feel his presence more than ever.

Tuesday, March 26, 2002

THIS MORNING I AM AGAIN GIVEN A VISION OF ROCHESTER. He is under our kitchen table lying down and facing the sink. This is a place he will occasionally go during the evening if he believes there is a mouse under the stove. This morning there is a shaft of sun or a heavenly light upon the beautiful marmalade fur on his small back. But it could not have been sun for no sun shines in the kitchen window due to the connecting screened-in-porch. He is glowing yet in a typical position. Both mornings he is as in reality, precious and handsome. I am overcome I should be shown him again, but cry and cry.

Wednesday, March 27, 2002

IT IS EARLY EVENING. I stand inside the front door having just come in from the screened-in-porch where I go occasionally for a breath of cold air and to say a prayer. I see Rochester again! He is just a foot or so ahead of me obviously having been outside too. He always came out on the porch with me. He is headed for the spot on the living room rug he likes, his coat shining and beautiful. I see him only from the back, a scene I have witnessed again and again, when he was here in body. In the blink of an eye he is gone. My heart stops and I cry.

Three gifts of three visions. Perhaps the key to being given these gifts is expectancy. Because I love him so deeply and we share one soul, I expect to see him and therefore I have. Or do my beliefs have nothing to do with these visions and they are pure gift?

Richard Bach has said—"*To bring anything into your life, imagine that it is already there.*"

Every day of my life since March 8th I have imagined Rochester to be here living as he always did with me but in a spiritual existence and form. Perhaps because I believe this unshakably I have been allowed these brief glimpses of my Angel. Perhaps others will doubt my sanity but I know he is here always, visions or not.

> *Millions of spiritual creatures*
> *Walk the earth*
> *Unseen, both when we wake, and*
> *When we sleep.*
> *What if earth and heaven*
> *Be to each other like*
> *More than on earth is thought?*

—Milton

It is Holy Week in the Christian faith—the week preceding Easter Sunday and Christ's resurrection from the dead on that day. Because Jesus lives—Rochester lives also.

Maundy Thursday
(In the Christian Faith)

Writing is scary, and its OK that it's scary,
that's part of what makes it so powerful and healing.
— Susan Zimmermann, *Writing to Heal the Soul*

Thursday, March 28, 2002

I READ WORDS OF ANOTHER that touch my soul concerning loss and death. The author states that we need to open ourselves to the memories and we will get the pain. I am opening myself continually. I am in pain. But too, I receive the devotedness and poignancy and sweetness of my little one throughout the days and nights. His dearness. His nearness. But the pain is ever there. His physical absence a mountain of pain.

I will just enter additional words of this same author here, thoughts that I have already written in these Journal pages in my own heart's words. For today, it is all I can write. My mind and heart are a mish-mosh of pain.

> *Understand that it is never over and done with. Don't look at healing as a process with a recognizable end—as if you take off the Band-Aid and oh! you're as good as new. We're never as good as new. We wouldn't want to be.*
>
> —Janet Sternburg, *Phantom Limb*

47

Writing is an internal *"journey"* that is freeing. It lets me *"travel"* in the pain discovering more and more. It honors Rochester as well. It is a *"passage"* I must make in a *"corridor"* of eternal time.

Bob and Rochester in times past
with a stack of my own completed journals, 1990

Good Friday
(In the Christian Faith)

There is not an animal on the earth, not a flying creature on two wings,
but they are people like unto you.

—The Koran

Friday, March 29, 2002

I BELIEVE WHEN WE GET TO HEAVEN we will be shown that our precious animal companions have been the glorious means for us, when they were on earth, to advance in spiritual holiness and in the life of self-giving and deep love.

Anyone who has ever had a deep relationship with an animal or has one now, has frequently experienced times when something exists between animal and human that defies explanation—from a dimension not known. And that experience may be often repeated but never less awesome. There comes the distinct feeling, an impression on one's soul, that a being or entity lives within the creature that seems divine. I personally have know this daily with my Rochester. I do so even after March 8th as I live with him each day in spirit, confirming all of these impressions I have had through the years in our love and relationship before March 8th.

Those who have experienced this will understand what I am saying. Therefore, can we risk ever doing anything to our animal companions that we would not want done to ourselves? Can we ever risk indifference and not love them with all our hearts as they should be loved? Have we

49

not all felt the pain of indifference from others at some point or points in time? I have. I could not ever bear for Rochester to ever have known that.

God who breathed the same breath of life into us, breathed the same breath of life into His creatures, and we are all God's creatures. I never felt above Rochester, in fact I knew he was sent to me as one *to look up to* for guidance and comfort, and for *rising* to a higher dimension. I spent every day in his presence loving, honoring, and appreciating him to the utmost. I would have done anything for him, and did. If I could have died in his place or with him, I would have. That is not bravado but my utmost truth. He was my Angel. He is my Angel forever.

Just as I have spent a Holy hour with our Lord today in remembrance as He died on the cross that we too may live and have eternal life with Him, so too I spend my Holy Hour with Rochester. Though I exist with him every moment in thought, prayer and deep grieving, today between five and six PM I will spend embracing Rochester in spirit in our writing room through that hour of agony.

THE ANGEL OF PATIENCE

To weary hearts, to mourning homes
God's meekest angel gently comes;
No power has he to banish pain,
Or give us back our lost again;
And yet in tenderest love, our dear
And heavenly Father sends him here.
There's quiet in the angel's glance,
There's rest in his still countenance!
He mocks no grief with idle cheer,
Nor wounds with words the mourner's ear
What ills and woes he may not cure
He kindly trains us to endure.

— John Greenleaf Whittier

Easter Sunday

A friend
Welded into our life is more to us
Than twice five thousand kinsmen,
one in blood.

—Euripedes

Sunday, March 31, 2002

IT IS EASTER SUNDAY and we attend St. Anthony of Padua parish in Sanbornville, New Hampshire fifteen minutes from our cottage in the woods of East Wakefield. Each Christmas and Easter for many years we have had flowers placed at the altar for our loved ones in Heaven. Their names have appeared in the Church Bulletins for that particular day. This year our donation covered a request for a new name to be added to our family of names of my parents, Bob's father, my uncle, and a mutual friend most dear. This Easter Rochester's name appears with these five names. We have listed him as Chester H. Kolb. The "H" is for Harry, Bob's love name for him. Bob feels people might recognize he is not a human if "Rochester" is used, but I know Father Edmund knows who he is. We have many times discussed Rochester, and Asta, his little dog. In November and December we also had poinsettias on the altar for our former neighbor's cat Alex, and our daughter and son-in-law's dog Friday. Memorials are lovingly needed beneath the altar and cross for precious animal companions too. It is comforting to see the lilies there but heartbreakingly unbelievable that one should be for my beloved little one. I take numerous Church Bulletins on the way out the door so that I may share them with family members as I always do. One announcement cut out from the Bulletin is to be glued in Rochester's Journal. Because Jesus lives, Rochester lives also.

Hallelujah!

The Weight of a Loss

I measure every Grief I meet
With narrow, probing Eyes—
I wonder if it Weighs like Mine—
Or has an Easier size.

—Emily Dickinson

Tuesday, April 2, 2002

THE DEATH OF EACH LOVED ONE IS UNIQUE and creates a grief unimaginable. It is without comparison, be it human or animal, and we all bear it and live with it in our own way and as best as we can. It seems things are constantly happening to either accentuate the grief or to point to it in some way. We are like open wounds expecting more pain and more blows upon our agony and vulnerability. The littlest occurrence or thought can cause us to cry without any warning.

And so it is unexpectedly warming to my wounded heart this morning when two instances occur to make me cry, yet also feel like I have comfort and extreme presence of Rochester. First I walk by the kitchen table and look at the spot on the end of it where Rochester laid so often while I cooked or addressed mail, or where he simply meditated. Instead of his precious body, a magazine lay open in his spot. I cannot imagine I have put it there. I keep the area open always for him even after March 8th.

I glance down at the open page, the front of the magazine folded under so as to expose this page. Immediately I see the name *"Rochester"* and I am taken back! I do a double take and look again. It is amazing! The word is not *"Rochester"* but *"Orchestra."* Because I am centered on my little one, all the letters of his name seem to light up and rearrange themselves so as to spell his name! I look closely. Is his name an anagram of *Orchestra?* Anagrams are something Bob and I enjoy discovering. How could we ever have missed this one so significant! Because I am so weak it seems now I deliberately go over the word, spelling out *"Rochester"* while staring at *"Orchestra."*

At last the truth is given up. It is not an anagram but is missing out on being one by only one letter. Instead of his name ending in "er"—in this case it is forced to end in "ar." It is missing one "e" and has instead an "a."

But it is lovely to realize that all these years I have experienced the music that Rochester put into my heart and soul by his very existence and his deep love, and it came close to truly being a full orchestra except for one letter. How very beautiful! However to me, he was always a complete and overflowing orchestra. He still is.

As if that is not enough to momentarily comfort, I turn on the TV to briefly receive some early morning news from CNN. The first words I hear are from Prince Charles of England commenting lovingly on the Queen Mother, his grandmother, who had died three days previous at the age of one hundred and one. The first words I hear him say bring tears for it is as if he is speaking of my Rochester as well. He says she was *"endearing"* and *"most magical"* and no truer statements could be made about Rochester. He also speaks of how her death leaves a *"chasm"* and I silently say *"yes"* through my tears. My little one was not royalty with a Kingdom as this great lady was, but an Angel who always seemed to make the Kingdom of Heaven very present. And now he awaits there to one day welcome us — as well as continues to guide us here on earth.

By Joy, Surprised

When you argue for your limitations,
all you get are your limitations.

—Dr. Wayne W. Dyer

Friday, April 5, 2002

MY DESIRE TO HAVE HIM BACK AGAIN on my lap, in my arms, in his daily play and activities, is constant and ongoing. Everything I do is related in my heart and mind to how it was when Rochester was right here visibly sharing life with me. But I am still rational yet overwhelmingly sad. I am not delusional with an overactive imagination. When I experienced the three visions of Rochester on three separate but consecutive days, though always open and expectant, I did not specifically anticipate them in any way. Because I miss him so, I was surprised by joy and appearances of him, beyond anything I could have hoped for in my own mind.

And so sitting upon the sofa tonight as I did always with Rochester, my back against the arm and my legs stretched down the cushions I hold my book and blankly stare ahead at the television. Bob is in his chair to my left. As if compelled I turn my head suddenly to the left, and there in a flash of marmalade color is Rochester's image behind Bob's chair. Then it is gone! I melt inside and I do not tell Bob. I thank God for this glimpse of assurance of my precious little love. That was last night. Tonight it happens again, exactly as before, one half hour later, and on the four week anniversary of his passing! His eyes hold me for a brief moment.

55

Shortly before his passing he stood in that very same spot on the floor behind the chair staring at me with his big golden eyes. It happened frequently, but that night I specifically remember. He truly wanted to look into my eyes, to have my attention. I looked into his eyes with great love until he released me. Perhaps these two new appearances are to remind me of that specific night—to give me his love anew. I believe so.

Last night it was four weeks ago I sat with him in my vigil through the night! He has bestowed on me gifts of his appearance on the anniversaries of the two most anguishing days of my existence and that changed my life.

Tears tumble from my eyes and I am so grateful. I say a prayer that this will always continue. I will always believe that it is possible and never shut down my expectancy or be told it cannot be.

St. Mark said, *"With God all things are possible."* That does not leave much out.

He stared at me with his big golden eyes

A New Dimension

Death ends a life but it does not end a relationship
—from the motion picture, *I Never Sang for My Father*

Saturday, April 6, 2002

THERE IS A QUOTATION THAT STATES THAT *"Death ends a life but it does not end a relationship."* Our relationship goes on with loved ones whether they are still alive or have died. Talk to the persons and dear animals in Heaven that you love as if they are alive and present with you, for they are! This can be done in prayer and in meditation, or in simple conversation as you go through your days. Or it can be done through writing in a journal. I do all of these to be with Chester.

The above quotation has had great meaning for me and is truth. Even though our beloved animal companions or humans can no longer be seen in ways as before, or touched, or hugged—they are there for us. And though this life as we knew it, their life—has ended, it still goes on in Heaven. When I write that now I feel ill inside and something happens within me. This feeling often washes over me and I feel so lost and helpless. But I believe with all my broken heart that our relationship, Rochester's and mine, still goes on and will never end throughout all eternity.

When I am quiet and listen I hear words from him. I write them down. I too have the comfort and joy of knowing that he can hear me and he does know what I am writing in my journal to him or about him. He can know my love directly in this way and hear my questions and know all that is in my heart just as he did when he was on earth. He answers me. I believe as a Christian we have this certainty and joy that if we are in Jesus our relationship with those we love does not end when one dies. I am sure this must be true in other religions too. Our relationship continues for all time, here and in the hereafter.

We can try to bring healing into our relationship also if there had been need of healing on our side—be it with a beloved animal or human. We can work out these things in our prayers and in our writing to them for they will hear and know. And if we had loose ends and everything was not neat and tidy between ourselves and our animal companion (or an individual) when they suddenly died, why we can do all that we possibly can to make it right from our perspective, and then in faith—we accept that it is accomplished. Through this we will have peace of heart and know that we are in complete love and resolution with this loved one just beyond the veil where we cannot visualize, but he or she can see and hear us.

I am eternally grateful that Rochester and I were continually in love and harmony, and our hours and years filled with the joy of being in each other's presence and company. We never showed each other anything but full respect and love, and our life together was a gift, and shall ever continue to be so in a new dimension. Our relationship has a life of its own—a blessed life.

When you go apart alone to think and pray and write and express your inner feelings, God is there with you and wonderful things happen gradually. Also you need silence in order to hear Him speak and you will be amazed at how you will look forward to those quiet moments as a listener, as well as actually praying and writing. I think He will whisper many secrets to you as will your animal companion, and when this happens write down the words. It happens—and when it does I write everything down I can quickly capture. I am keeping a special journal. I am so thankful I have always written Rochester's messages to me, not just the ones since March 8th. It is almost as if "*writing*" is a separate form of angel, or a gift from the angels, one given to me as a little child that has seen me through many extremely difficult passages of life. This present passage is most difficult of all—for so many reasons.

Forever Together

Yes, we have this assurance. Those who belong to God shall live again
—Isaiah 26:19 Living Bible (The Way)

Sunday, April 7, 2002

I KNOW THERE ARE MANY CHRISTIANS and others who find it painful that they will never see their beloved animal companions again, because that is what they were taught to believe, or it was a definite feeling that they acquired from many sources. I say to you now, so that you may cast this old belief away; rejoice, that you *will* have your dear animal with you in Heaven.

As Christians, we are baptized in water and by the Spirit, and we have the Holy Spirit within us as our Paraclete and Advocate and Guide. I believe the Holy Spirit speaks to each of us and convicts us on matters in our own lives and of spiritual matters and concerns in the world, and I believe we must listen to Him. When He impresses things on our soul, we must be attentive—or, if need be, *act*. And there is an inner knowing when this happens to us, that the Holy Spirit is impressing and directing us. Often we are never the same when a Holy thought has made its mark upon our soul, for it can change a belief, alter one's life, cause one to speak out—and yet in all of these leave us with a peace and certainty within. He will not leave doubt, for God is not a God of confusion (1 Corinthians 14 : 33) but one of peace. And so we must listen to what the Holy Spirit is saying to us within—and when He speaks to us, *believe!*

59

And then—do not let anyone thereafter shake our belief in what has been impressed on our soul.

I have had major changes in my life occur in this way. I have recognized the Holy Spirit's voice and calling and I could not doubt! And despite all outward circumstances that would contradict and try to say otherwise, I would know that what I heard within was the directive I must follow. When one hears the Holy Spirit's voice—and obeys—one cannot go back to what was before.

I share this here (and many other things in great depth on this subject in my book, *Compassion for All Creatures*) to emphasize that once I had the inner conviction from the Holy Spirit that animals and all God's creatures do inhabit Heaven with us, then I could never believe otherwise. It was irrevocable! No matter what anyone else may argue, I cannot be shaken on this.

In a wonderful and loving book, entitled *Dog Miracles—Inspirational and Heroic True Stories* by well known authors Brad Steiger and Sherry Hansen Steiger, they state:

> *Our own research conducted over these past nearly 45 years has convinced us that just as there is life after death for humans, so also do our pets exist on the Other Side. Just as dogs are our constant, loving companions in the material world, so do our spiritual essences remain connected beyond the grave. It may well be that dogs will be numbered among our best friends in heaven, as well as on Earth.*

And I would add too that cats and other beloved animal companions will be there also. I am honored to be quoted on this very subject of Animals in Heaven in this inspiring book, *Dog Miracles*, and in the rereading of this book in this present difficult time I have been given solace. Brad and Sherry also state, *"We have received hundreds of reports from serious-minded men and women who claim to have been visited by the spirits of their beloved canine companions."* This comforts me and confirms my own visits from Rochester since March 8th.

I would like to share with you a scripture verse that has great meaning to me in many areas of my life. In this present sad time of longing for the physical presence of Rochester, it is especially supportive. The verse is Hebrews 11:1 and I will again use the Living Bible (the Way), for

I feel this paraphrase is incredibly filled with encouragement and hope, compared to other translations.

> *What is faith? It is the confident assurance that something we want is going to happen. It is the certainty that what we hope for is waiting for us, even though we cannot see it up ahead.*

Now you who long to know that your animal companions will share heaven with you—apply this verse to this longing, and claim it by faith right now. The entire chapter of Hebrews 11 speaks of the faith of the men and women of old, and we are to have the same faith in our lives, despite circumstances around us that may indicate otherwise, and despite the words of others who would have us believe as they do and try to shake our faith. If God did all these things that are listed and more, including bringing women's sons back from the dead because these women had the faith that He would, then how could we believe otherwise—that He has not intended our beloved animal companions and creatures of the world that He created to share Heaven with us. Why would a merciful God, who asks us to have faith for all things unseen (reread Hebrews 11:1) and a certainty and an assurance, cut down His own creatures and let their wonderful lives end in nothingness? I can never accept that—nor can other Christians and those of other faiths who believe as I do and in a merciful God. If Rochester is not in heaven then I do not want to be there either. I would rather be with him in nothingness—for he is far more deserving of Heaven than am I and I would not want to be where he is not.

So many other things can be considered that will help you to know that your beloved animals will share heaven with you. First of all, God created the animals, made them in harmony with the universe, and said they were good. Not only that, but He created them for Himself. Scripture supports this also. In the story of creation, we can see the high regard God has for the animals, for their creation immediately followed man's, and they were made out of the same ground as man. I believe animals have a divine purpose in the universe, since God often chose them to be messengers. Also animals inspire others and cause a deep love for God. I know this by the way that love and prayers well up in me when I look at my Rochester. They have since he was a kitten and always shall. I am eternally grateful for this little beloved being in my life.

Always those who live with animal companions know their intelligence and emotions and their unconditional love. Their company often proves finer than that of humans. Their comfort is incomparable. I am in the holiest and finest of company with Rochester since he entered my life, and too in this new dimension of living now that we share.

Books by Cleveland Amory, well known author and animal rescuer, that I own and reread, have touched millions of hearts through stories about his life with his cat *"Polar Bear."* He has authored *The Cat Who Came for Christmas, The Cat and the Curmudgeon, The Best Cat Ever* and *Ranch of Dreams.* Why do people from various walks of life feel they need to give such dignity and love to their animals by immortalizing them in *"dedications"* and in entire books? It is because they have found them worthy and filled with the traits that ennoble and enrich our lives. And this is so because our dear companions have souls, and they truly will share Heaven with us. Never, as I wrote these words before for my *Compassion for All Creatures* and so many additional thoughts on Heaven and animals, did I ever think I would be writing them anew because my little Rochester had gone to Heaven. Never, as I have written earlier, did I ever think we would be separated! I believed simply that we would forever remain together until we both went to Heaven. That was my belief and gave me strength in the life I lived daily with my precious little angel. There is no rationality to it. I just believed it with all my heart. Obviously the eventual obvious was blotted from my mind because I could not even bear to think of Rochester and me being separated, whether I be taken first or him. We simply would always remain together here and in Heaven. And Bob also. Obviously I was not in charge despite all my prayers and undying belief in this fact. But we *are* together forever, just presently not as I hoped or ever planned. I sit here in tears as I write so I can barely see.

Perhaps the words of a special friend of ours, Daniel T. Deane, Jr. of Wyncote, Pennsylvania, will help us all. They are the closing words to an incredibly beautiful and long testimony of faith written by him in my *Compassion for all Creatures.* May Dan's thoughts and words be added here to bring further faith and hope to all those who know and believe that they will be in Heaven with their beloved animal companions.

I tend to believe that one day, in God's Heaven, we will again hug our cherished pet animals, ride on the backs of winged horses, and walk up to both the lamb and the lion and playfully scratch them behind their ears.

In his hand is the soul of every living thing, and the life breath of all mankind.

—Job 12

Rev. Billy Graham also has given a statement that I only recently learned, but had I not read it my beliefs were strong and present before discovering it. It confirms all that I believe and have written in my previous book and in this entry.

Heaven is the place of final and complete happiness God has prepared for us—and if animals are necessary to make us happy in heaven, then you can be sure God will have them there.

Evening of same day, April 7

ONIGHT IN A FLASH OF CLARITY I see Rochester jump up on the striped chair he loves in the living room as I sit near by on the sofa. I see his dear rear legs that were always so handsome to me, his tail high, and he faces away from me. It is as clear of him as in reality before March 8th. My heart stops. I sit immobile. He vanishes. I cry. I am so grateful for these gifts of his visible presence!

Grieving

With silence as their benediction
God's angels come
When in the shadow of a great affliction,
the soul sits dumb.

—John Greenleaf Whittier

Wednesday, April 10, 2002

To MOST HUMANS WHO LOVE AN ANIMAL and have shared their daily lives with a beloved one, when death comes to this companion, it is as crushing and heartbreaking as if a human has died. It can even be more so! To those who have no animals, this may seem absolutely incredible, and they may even think it wrong. It is not! An animal gives utter love and devotion day in and day out, whereas often humans fail us. Yes they do! To one especially who lives alone with an animal companion or who spends hours alone with an animal companion, and they belong to each other exclusively, this is even more tragic to the human who is left alone. I am not saying that this death is more devastating than any other—though to me and to many others it may be, just that the human involved may need considerable help and consolation. But any death of an animal is unbearable to one who deeply loves their beloved companion.

When anyone remarks to one who has lost an animal friend, *"You can always get another one,"* or *"It was only a pet,"* the speaker is indeed showing no understanding and will certainly add additional pain to the bereaved person. I have had an extremely painful thing written to me concerning God and Rochester's passing that made me both dissolve, and too, be inwardly angry. It was made by a Christian who disregards animals, and it was this belief stated, so completely opposite from mine, that stung so. Animal owners often are looked upon as completely strange if they are in grief over their loss. Yet the same people who thus add pain would probably have much compassion if the loss were one of a human family member or friend. In our society, grief over an animal is often unacceptable behavior, and the people who are suffering have to suppress their grief, feel embarrassment over tears, and often must stay away from friends as much as possible. The animal-human bond is an incredibly strong one and not many understand this unless it has been within one's personal experience or within the life of a close friend or family member. From this moment on, however, if you have not realized all of this before and have been insensitive to others concerning the death of animal friends, please pray that you will no longer treat this lightly or utter words that may sear the heart of the human who is experiencing the loss. I believe any veterinarian would speak these same words, as well as anyone involved with animals in any way.

In a recent late night interview with author Dominick Dunne, he stated that *"after a few weeks you are on your own. People cannot stand your grief any longer."* His grief is for his kidnapped and murdered daughter some years ago. If he has experienced this terrible and crushing insensitivity in regard to his human loved one, then how very often and much more so is this insensitivity for a beloved animal.

It is important to know that it is normal and right to grieve over our animal companions, and if necessary surround yourself with other humans who understand and care, who can give emotional support. If you are like myself you prefer to be alone in the days and weeks following your companion's passing, or with your closest human such as husband or wife who also love your dear companion. Avoid human friends who simply minimize your heartbreak. Taking time to grieve is necessary for anyone suffering a loss, be it animal or human. Grieving happens powerfully and spontaneously when you love deeply, without choosing to specifically do it. It cannot be helped! Some may want to talk with friends who also have experienced the loss of a dear creature in their lives, for they will best understand and be better able to support, counsel, and lead you through your grief. It may even be necessary to talk with your veterinarian alone, or a counselor—or perhaps your minister, priest, or other religious leader, provided they love and respect animals.

Connie, a close friend of mine with an enormous, compassionate heart and who has rescued cats for years, sent me both a beautiful bouquet of flowers immediately after Chester left, and a recent article concerning bereaved pet owners. The flowers are still in our living room and the article arrived as I was writing this chapter. Connie has grieved deeply for her beloved cats. This article tells of a support group in New Jersey for people grieving the death of their animal companions. The participants are men, women and children and they can attend a single season or attend for months. They will be with people who understand their deep loss and why they grieve and who are sympathetic listeners. They are told by their leader that their animal companion will always be with them and that the relationship has shifted from physical to spiritual.

One man, seated with his wife and reminiscing about their beloved dog, told the group—*"I've lost parents, a brother, both grandparents. This has hit us harder,"* he said. *"A lot of people don't get it, when you try to relate how you bonded with an animal. It's nice to have a group of people who get it."* This couple attends the support group regularly since the death of their much loved dog. Here the people in grief can talk about everything concerning death and grieving, and share pictures and stories about their sweet animals. They do not have to fear they will be laughed at. I am certain there must be other groups like this in other states and there are pet loss hot lines with professional grief counsellors.

When I was twenty-one, my new husband Bob of seven months was forced to leave me. He was in the Navy and we were in San Diego and his ship was going to Japan. I was seven months pregnant and devastated at the separation. When I see men on the news leaving for Afghanistan and some returning after months of being overseas, I understand the pain of separation these couples are feeling and have felt. The baby girl that was born to us during those months he was away is now married with six children of her own as we had, but I will always remember those difficult months. While Bob was gone I kept with me a pair of pajamas and an old shirt he had worn immediately before he left—and took them back to Pennsylvania with me when he sailed off. These articles carried his scent and were comforting while he was gone. Reading recently a book on grieving, the woman author mentioned how she wore an old shirt of her deceased husband's because of his scent still upon it, and I understood.

I have a comfort object also connected with Rochester, a comforter. Interestingly it is usually a blanket or comforter a young child remains attached to for their personal comforting and in order to be able to sleep. I am still a child inside and very much in need of comforting now. The comforter I write about was personally made for me some years ago by our daughter Janna and is a lovely patchwork quilt of wildlife animals. It is pictured in several of my books and always with my dear little Rochester lying in its depths. I folded it in quarters making it extra thick and placed it on the bed next to my desk. It was in the center of this quilt Chester would lay keeping me company as I wrote and occasionally taking a nap. The quilt remains on the bed as I write now. Everything is the same except he is invisible. But I know his spirit rests in the center of that quilt every day as always, and so that comforter continues to give me great personal comfort. Each morning before I begin to write I place a small pouch containing his soft marmalade fur on one far corner, and his purple collar with tags on the other far corner.

Each evening after I complete my writing I kneel down beside the bed and pray, and in tears I put my face into the quilt so as to absorb his precious scent that is still strongly but delicately there. He always had a beautiful scent. I am overcome by it no matter how many times I do it. He is ever, ever with me. Little airy pieces of his fur lay there also. It is then I retrieve his pouch of fur and his purple collar and take them downstairs with me to place on my night table.

Too, I have a white quilted bathrobe that long ago he became fond of. Because I am always warm I never wear the robe, but I would lay it down the length of my legs as I sat on the sofa in the evenings and also in bed when I slept. Rochester would curl up on my legs or tummy and enjoy the softness of the robe as well. I washed it about a week before he left and long enough before for him to have left his imprint of scent. I fold it gently during the days to retain his loveliness within and unfold it only in the evenings so his spirit may lie upon it as his sweet body once did for so many years. Precious rituals like this help to keep sanity in the hearts and minds of loved ones left behind. Perhaps they are strange to some but overwhelmingly appreciated by others.

To be left behind is not something we are prepared for. Even though it was never part of the plan to outlive Rochester whom we love so, (no, as I have written elsewhere I thought we three would pass away together) or a person we love, it does in an unexpected way become our gift to the beloved one. It is we, instead of our precious one, who are experiencing the deep sorrow and the pain. Gladly I do this though so deeply in anguish, for I would do anything for him and would never want my little one to experience it. Animals do grieve deeply and often die of grief. However, if I could have my deepest wish come true—it would be what is expressed in this small verse—my wish from my grieving heart.

> If memories and tears could build a staircase,
> And grief a footpath or upward lane—
> I would climb at once to Heaven,
> And in my arms bring you home again.

When a loved one dies we have lost a part of ourselves. An enormous part. I can validate that most sincerely. In order to survive and get through our days and nights we create our own reality, our own little world. In the initial shock we begin to do this in order to make it through it all. Then in order to survive we do it differently as we attempt to devise new ways in which to live and go on in a new dimension with our beloved one.

Never judge a person that is grieving. You may think you understand but each is individual—and no one can tell another that they must stop.
—Unknown

When your heart is broken it's hard to feel blessed and protected. All your love energy, all your heart energy leaks out through the break line. You don't feel loved, protected, and guided. You feel drained, tired, exhausted and helpless.
—Melody Beattie, *Finding Your Way Home (A Soul Survival Kit)*

Mourning

MOURNING ROCHESTER

Today the loons return.
Their wails so other-worldly
cross the lake
as if for his sake—
And meet my silent wails
flung to the sky.
They rise and storm the heavens
and scream "Why?"

—JGK

Friday, April 12, 2002

TODAY THE LOONS RETURN and to hear their first wail, particularly across the lake at night, is an experience we await each year. They spend from April 'til late fall here on our lake and then winter on the Maine coast by the Atlantic Ocean. Today their wails add to my despair and sadness yet I am thankful they are back. We feel so fortunate to have their presence, a blessing through the years. How uncanny they should return on a Friday to seemingly help me to express the wails of sorrow within myself—remembering always the Friday Rochester went to Heaven.

Many birds are returning to our lake and to our own deck, birds we enjoy and await and that I continually take pictures of and write about. Every day Bob fills our many hanging feeders on the deck and also keeps the suet holder well stocked for the Hairy and Downy Woodpeckers that are constant visitors. This week, for the third time only since we have owned this cottage, we hear the unusual sounds of the large Pileated Woodpecker who has made rectangular holes in some of our trees. It is an honor to have this unusual bird visit. Like all the others arriving, I feel there is a special assemblage this year to honor Rochester.

Beside the dear Chickadees and Nuthatches, the Woodpeckers, Blue Jays, and other hardy birds who spend the winter with us, we are observing new varieties and old friends each morning. It is still too early in the season for many of the glorious birds to be with us yet, but already we have quite a gathering.

The Blue Heron returns to the cove and has been out front on the beach. And new first time visitors drop by for a surprising visit! Eight Wild Turkeys spend time below the deck on the lawn quite visible through our long sliding glass doors and for Rochester's spirit to enjoy as always.

Mourning Doves which I admire for their shyness and gentleness are here and they are particularly significant to me regarding Rochester. They are long time acquaintances of his and my heart feels their hearts are mourning his physical presence yet know he is there as always.

The Mallards I have written about often in my other books, and they too have entertained Rochester through the glass or screens for years. They spend most of the day (several couples) on our deck and occasionally fly down to the lake. It is mating season and there is pairing off. One year we witnessed a mating in front of our dock of a lovely bird we simply call "Mrs. Mallard," and a male. I wrote of this in my *Journal of Love*. These same Mallards knock on our glass doors upon arrival so we will know they are there and come out with some bread. Though there is plenty of seed in feeders and fallen on the deck for ground feeders, the bread is still a treat.

All of these birds are coming to call daily, the new ones and the regulars, with many more due. But this March and April I believe there is a special knowing amongst them that their friend Rochester who always gently observed them (and very close up) is very appreciative of their presence, and somehow in a spiritual dimension of God's creation, the birds' are honoring and able to see Rochester's spiritual presence, and he them, of course. There is definitely something going on that is celebrating Rochester and blessing us.

And what is more—there is a mystery most astounding that confirms all that I feel and am trying to express—and *that* is the *"mystery of the Crows."* We have many Crows in our woods and we have been entertained again and again by their rhythmic caws. The caws are delivered in a series of threes, fours, fives or more, and responses come in the same way. The cawing is loud and a definite communication is continual, and it is fascinating. The Crows seem so large at times I wonder they take flight. But a most mysterious visitation is occurring since Rochester abides here in spirit.

Since the weekend of March 9th and 10th following the sad, sad day of March 8th, we have two Crows with us always. At first there was mainly one, then the second one arrived. They have remained and are on our deck every day. They come and go briefly, but usually separately, and immediately return. One is usually always on patrol on our railing just sunning or eating. They look in our front windows, and when I am writing upstairs at my desk they often sit on the wooden bar holding the feeders and stare in at me there.

This is extraordinary, for no Crow has ever come on our deck with the smaller birds before in all the years we have owned this cottage and lived here. They always fly about in the woods and sit in the trees or walk on the lawn or beach. Never on our deck!

There are two amazing true stories I have read regarding birds that have come to mind these past days and weeks because of these two Crows. One story is "The Judgement of the Birds" by writer and naturalist Loren Eiseley, and the other author I do not know, but it is in regard to Sea Gulls keeping a vigil. In both cases the birds were acting out their mourning for a bird through gatherings and vigils. They are precious though sorrowful happenings, and show the great caring and compassion of these creatures in the natural world. They are haunting as are the two crows on our front deck and the vigil they are keeping. I believe with a certainty the Crows are there to honor and mourn Rochester, having been called in an other-worldly way we cannot know but only observe in awe. For six weeks these two birds are ever present to us on our deck making themselves very known by their actions and caws, and even their staid stance and silence at times. American Crows are among the most intelligent of birds.

At first I was so surprised through my tears to see two Crows there, for it was a first! Then, day after day they appeared as if called by a mysterious voice or sounding trumpet. And six weeks later they continue to keep vigil!

It has been so constant and unfailing I began to look up information on crows—not in the usual bird books but in ones I own about Native American lore. I truly feel these two Crows have a deep spiritual meaning in Rochester's regard and it is most comforting. I feel they are messengers. I am also praying for more insight.

Author Brad Steiger has written about "Crows" in his book, *Totems—The Transformative Power of Your Personal Animal Totem*. Much excellent information is given but several lines in particular struck me. He states that a Crow "*is one that watches shrewdly over the lay of the land on both spiritual and physical levels*" and too, that he "*expresses a point of view that touches several dimensions.*" Brad states, "*As you learn how to listen, you will find that he is a messenger without peer*" and too "*as a spirit helper, the Crow will be able to get you in touch with many ancient mysteries.*" The Crow is one of Brad's totem animals.

I feel so encouraged by this knowledge and will listen intently each day to these messengers out on our deck. Believing they are here because of Rochester, I will faithfully observe and record their actions. My journal already contains passages about them because I have felt all along they have come to us because of our beloved little Chester. Perhaps in time I will be shown more. I am so grateful. I have always felt that birds are God's messengers and now this is being shown to me in a constant, unfailing pattern of presence of two of His creatures, creatures so large they are approximately Rochester's size. I am waiting, and anticipate.

I am reminded that I made a drawing of a Crow for my book, *Compassion for All Creatures*, and originally this drawing was used in the front of a book authored by a poet and dear friend of mine, Dr. Francis J. McGeary. I have written about him in each of my own books. He requested I draw this Crow to appear on a front page of his book to express the title and contents. It is a large drawing of a Crow with head turned looking back on a tree branch in contrast to the same Crow in

much smaller size in my own book. How strange that it is a Crow and now they are appearing to me daily! I feel this same crow should appear on this page also to honor Rochester as the alive crows are doing.

Years ago I wrote a poem about Rochester titled "Travelling Ambassador" (of how he travelled very frequently from Pennsylvania to New Hampshire), and because it is long and has appeared in my book *Compassion* I will just close this meditation with the last lines, for they tell of Rochester's love of bird watching and why I wish now to share about the birds at this sad time.

> For soon he'll be where he loves most
> The little cottage where he's host—
> To birds and wildlife, who will stare
> Through screens and windows for they care,
> That Rochester has returned once more,
> The little goodwill ambassador.

Dedicated to   JGK
Rochester Harry Whittier Kolb
Famous Feline Traveler

If men had wings and bore black feathers, few of them would be clever enough to be crows.

—Rev. Henry Beecher Ward

> *Hope is the thing with feathers—*
> *That perches in the soul—*

—Emily Dickinson

Expectancy

This fifty-year-old woman was being propelled forward
in this youthful dash, like the older Margot Fonteyn
dancing with the twenty-year-old Nureyev.
It was as if this boy and I were now a single being,
whose heart and lungs were so strong we could go on indefinitely,
as if I had a new, permanent, and internal dance partner.

—A Change of Heart—a memoir,
Claire Sylvia with William Novak

Sunday, April 14, 2002

TONIGHT AS I AM PRAYING and thinking of my little Rochester something forcibly comes to mind that I had not thought about in some months. Though for a long period of time I had thought about it a great deal, that had not been so recently. Now here it was again and I instantly understood why.

Back in January 2001 I read a book that just left me in awe. It affected me so deeply I needed to have someone with whom to discuss it and asked Bob to read it. Since we rarely read the same books and enjoy books of totally different genres than the other, he was nice enough to make a concession. I wanted to question him continually as he read but I let him read it completely before we had our discussion. He was equally as floored by this story as I was, a true account of a woman who had had a heart and lung transplant in 1988 at the age of forty-eight in order to save her life from a rare lung disease.

Eventually we gave the book to many family members and friends because it was compelling and gave an extraordinary message. The opening quotation is from this book by and about a woman named Claire Sylvia.

This woman had her chest sawed open and her diseased organs cut out in order to undergo this incredible operation. In the place of her diseased heart and lungs, the heart and lungs of an eighteen year old man were grafted in their place. He had just died in a motorcycle accident. She thought then the greatest adventure of her life was finally over—but actually it was just beginning.

Even while in Intensive Care in recovery she began to feel the presence of something or someone else within her. At first terrified and then absorbed and fascinated, she realized her tastes, habits and attitudes had changed. She had new food cravings. She began to act with impetuosity and aggressiveness, behavior she had never shown. She was drawn to cool colors instead of vibrant ones—and five months after the operation she had a remarkable dream. In this dream she met a man named Tim L., a man she absolutely believed was her donor.

The second part of her journey was to confirm whether or not the new personality within her was actually the donor. During all of this passage she struggles with timeless questions most profound: Where does body end and spirit begin? Is it possible to live on after death? Claire eventually learns some of the answers she has been looking for. She comes to understand the surprising bequest of love from the dead to the living. These are just some of the things spoken of on the cover of the book and then revealed fully within the pages. Possible answers are given to some of life's deepest mysteries. It gives comforting ways of accepting our mortality and gives great light to our dark tragedies.

It is a story and example of how cellular memory can outlive physical death. I recommend it.

And so tonight this book comes to mind and I realize why.

This woman received many new experiences into her life after being the recipient of another's heart and lungs. I believe I am the carrier and receptacle for Rochester's breath and soul, his Anima, and I am learning more about the Holy meaning of this as each day passes. I will share more about this with you in a later entry. I believe I will continue to be shown, that *"there is more."* It is quite possible that the visions of Rochester given me here in our cottage, are part of this great mystery. I must remain expectant, yet live with the absolute certainty and faith just as I have been doing, that even if there is not another vision, that he is ever here with me. I can never be shaken on that! It is my hope and sanity until we are together in Heaven. I sense him, talk to him, feel his presence as we go through our days and nights, and live as if he is here, because he is. Amen!

The Fairy Ring

Music I heard with you was more than music—
— Conrad Aiken

You're the music, the laughter, the fun in my life!
My heart does a little dance each time I think of you.
— Unknown

Tuesday, April 16, 2002

*M*USIC CAN HAVE SUCH AFFECT ON US that we can often desire it deeply, choosing selections for our moods and needs. Then there are times when the slightest strains can be invasive. I am experiencing the latter these past weeks and deliberately play no music of any kind. In the times in the evening when the television is on, the merest lovely notes from a program or commercial can dissolve me into tears.

Rochester and I had a song that was ours. Years ago in 1989 a close friend Ruth gave me a cassette tape brought back from her vacation in Acadia National Park, where she had first heard the music and been overwhelmed by its beauty. She bought a cassette for each of us and I have been ever grateful. This music has calmed my soul and Rochester's, and receiving that tape began a portion of my life that was so precious, for the music became *"our song—our music."* It has no words only supernaturally beautiful strains and is most other-worldly. It is called *"The Fairy Ring"* by Mike Rowland.

From the time I first listened to it and been so deeply moved by it, it became *"our song."* Rochester and I listened to it each night before sleep and I have played it continually since 1989. It is not music to read by or write by or use as background. It is for us, music for the night and aloneness, and shared only with Rochester and Bob. It did not appeal to Bob after many playings, (and even originally, but he thought it would eventually end and I would stop playing it.) Thirteen years later it was still playing each night, but in all fairness he goes to sleep so quickly he does not realize it is on.

I know only that the haunting strains were so healing to me through the years and to Rochester also. I have written about it in detail in other books. It especially calmed and soothed Chester after our 430-mile trips we would make so frequently back and forth to New Hampshire in the years before 1996.

I long to hear this music now for it may bring unexpected solace as it has done in other situations, but I am afraid to play it. And so since the night of March 8th when I returned to our cottage with empty arms, I ceased to play the music that was ours. The quietness at night before sleep is so deep without these gentle strains I played so softly for us. He would put his little white paws into my hands as he and I drifted off to sleep. I can barely write this now to tell you for I cannot see.

In these weeks the silence is so painful. I pray in various ways and close with the Rosary, and know that he is touching it at times with one paw as we hold hands. In time I will be strong enough to play the tape. Bob has made so many extra copies of it through the years for we kept wearing it out and could never find another in a store. The cassette sits in the player waiting to be heard. Perhaps soon.

After silence, that which comes nearest to expressing the inexpressible is music.

—Aldous Huxley

Rochester Lives

I have put my spirit within you, and you shall live—

—Ezekiel 37:14

Friday, April 19, 2002

Dear Rochester —

It is Friday again
Each one I dread.
Six weeks ago Friday
They pronounced you dead.

I live out the days
As if in a dream —
But inside myself
I scream and scream.

JGK

GOD IS THE SOURCE OF ALL life and despite my despair He is our Creator, and Rochester and I are united as one eternally in Him. It is our comfort and hope in our present physical separation. My broken heart hears this message but brokenness remains. It is the second time this message comes to me in three days.

79

Parable of the Pennies

My sheep hear my voice. I know them, and they follow me.
I give them eternal life.

—Jesus (John 10: 25, 27, 28)

Sunday, April 21, 2002

BOB DRIVES OUT OF THE WOODS and into the corner store today to get a Sunday News published by the Union Leader. I sit on the sofa in utter stillness not moving until he returns. I have been crying many times this morning and feel so helpless. Precious memories keep surfacing. Once home, Bob says he has a present for me and tells me he found three pennies on the ground outside the store. He believes they have meaning for me. He knows how I think. The symbolic is hidden in the seemingly ordinary for me. Immediately I tell him they represent Rochester, him, and myself. The shiny penny is Rochester, always radiant and innocent, the other two are us. The same shine is not there.

These pennies do have meaning to me. There they were separated on the ground and to all appearances lost to the owner. Rochester and Bob and I have become physically separated and I feel so lost, yet God gathers us up with His mighty hand and we are forever united in Him in spirit—and united one day in Heaven. We three belong to Him. As Bob collects the pennies and then hands them to me between his thumb and finger in a tight togetherness as one, so God too keeps us tightly together as one—even though we seem outwardly separated now.

And yet—my insides sink and turn over and seemingly fall apart all in an instant a dozen times a day when certain moments come to mind and I cannot see Rochester.

... when certain moments come to mind ...

Memories of Rochester when he was a kitten on the retreat with me in our cottage in September 1986

A Beloved Portrait

IMAGINING

A portrait painted
　　in the past
Its subject sainted
　　and held fast
　　　　within my being—
Becomes an icon
　　just in the seeing.

Imagining, — I reach
　　inside the frame,
Hold him again
　　and whisper softly
　　　　now his name —

　"Rochester"

—JGK

Monday April 22, 2002

ONCE UPON A TIME my daughter Barbara painted a portrait of Rochester and surprised me with this precious gift. It was painted during his first year of life. He is lying on a colorful small crocheted afghan that

82

was atop a bureau that he liked to lie on. She presented it to me immediately after completing it and I have treasured it. It is framed in a gold frame and matted in burgundy, and is twenty inches by ten inches. It has been displayed various places during the years both in our former home in Pennsylvania and in our cottage here. For the past several years it has been hanging above a shelf made by Bob that is on top of the windows in the back bedroom. This room is across the small landing at the top of the living room stairs from my writing room, my room in which Barbara stays when she visits. Since I always had the precious living Rochester in the front room with me, I had placed his portrait in the nearby back room.

Today I go into the back room as I do daily for some paper and my entire being is drawn to the portrait of Chester. It happens each time I enter the room.

Today I remove the portrait from the wall and take it downstairs and temporarily stand it on the floor to lean against the television. I sit on the sofa to stare at it but cannot see it for my tears.

If only he could be that kitten again. If only I could reach over the frame's threshold and in reality stroke his precious fur and body, and kiss his forehead. I already have smothered the canvas with kisses. If only I could lift him from that frame and cuddle him in my arms. Despair washes over me and I am lost in memories, and longing to hold him close and never let him go.

There are six other prized pieces of Barbie's art on the stairs, in the living room and adjoining kitchen area, but I realize I need *this* painting before me daily. With extremely limited wall space in this cottage I do some rearranging to create the perfect space for it next to the bookshelf and directly in my line of vision whenever I am in the room. And as I sit on the sofa at night with legs stretched down the length, my back against the arm, I will have Rochester on my legs in spirit always sound asleep, and my kitten Rochester in the portrait before me.

How grateful I am to Barbie for painting this portrait for it is not only a treasure and a joy but truly a spiritual icon. An icon participates in *"the energies of Christ"* and it is advised to stand before an icon and close our eyes before starting to pray. I do. An icon is a sign of God's presence and we are helped to pray by simply being in its presence. I am. An icon, like the painting of Rochester, acts as a revelation of the nature of the Divine.

For when I look at Rochester, I experience my dearest and deepest spiritual encounters.

He is filled with God. When Rochester's and my eyes meet—the Angels sing. It has always been so and ever shall be.

Portrait of Rochester painted by Barbara Jan Egan

Impression of Love

No day is lived in vain, if I but cherish someone else's presence.

—Unknown

Wednesday, April 24, 2002

LOVE'S IMPRINT

In spirit now you lie on me
And I still know that gentle touch—
The imprint of your preciousness.
Although I cannot visibly see
Your dear, sweet body curled in sleep
      upon my lap —
And though I weep
      in longing —
We are forever one.
      I do not need to see.
        I love, I trust,
          I know.

JGK

DAY AND NIGHT I experience Rochester's imprint of love upon my heart and soul and mind, and too upon my lap, and stretched out legs upon the length of the sofa or in bed. It is real, and intensely warm, and I am blessed. Because I desire his presence so, and continually thank him for being with me as before, he is. He is very evident to my spirit.

Gifts from
Our Loved Ones

Keep some souvenirs of your past,
or how will you ever prove it wasn't all a dream?

—Ashleigh Brilliant

Thursday April 25, 2002

TODAY I RECEIVE AN E-MAIL from a young woman acquaintance of mine with whom I have exchanged two previous E-mails. We have never met. She is the daughter of the man whose name is on the silver cuff bracelet I have had on my left arm since January without removing. The official title is a Mercy B.A.N.D. (Bearing Another's Name Daily) and I have written of it in an earlier entry. She has special news to tell me. Her Mother in New York has received a letter telling her that her husband's wallet and cards have been found at the site of the World Trade Center disaster. Their daughter writes that her brother is going to New York to get their father's wallet. She and her brother live in New England. This letter is overwhelming to them for they feel now that their father was not burned, yet not with a certainty. The news touched me so deeply. I pray for Edward and his family every day and today tears came again imagining anew what they have been going through since September 11th.

Their son will be given a wallet—and I was handed a purple collar with tags, all that remains from the former bodies of our beloved ones. Yes, we each have other belongings of the ones we dearly love, but none so significantly personal and saturated in sorrow as those handed to us after death. They are sacramentals, a part or essence of each loved one, a carrier of each presence.

Friday's Grief – Friday's Gifts

For Rochester

A faithful friend is an image of God.

—French Proverb

Friday, April 26, 2002

EACH FRIDAY IS LIKE A KNIFE IN THE HEART. Images rise up of that one Friday that took my little love from my life in the precious form that I used to hold in my arms. The little one who gave of himself to me everyday of his life and brought such joy.

Today he arranges with the Angels (for he is one himself) to have two cartons delivered to our cottage by United Parcel Service. I believe that with all my heart! For them to arrive on a Friday is a personal sign and message to me that Rochester is aware and part of my life always. The cartons contain my latest and newest published book *Beneath the Stars and Trees—there is a place,* and Rochester was with me in our writing room as I wrote every word; inspiring me, communicating with me, and loving me. It is his book as much as it is mine. How I wish his real presence that I can hug and hold is present to see these books. But his spirit is, just as it is within all the pages of every book.

Because I know a special tribute I wrote and his picture is in the book in regard to March 8th, I cannot look at the books at this time. I let Bob open the carton and he takes a book out to keep beside his chair to browse in this evening. But he does pause to admire the cover now and

89

glance within the pages. He tells me everything is beautiful and that Chester's tribute is there and very wonderful. Chester is written about and pictured throughout the entire book but it is this tribute that keeps me from the book now. I never dreamed he would not be physically by my side as always to see our books when they arrived.

Later from 5 to 6 PM I spend an hour in prayer and meditation as I do every Friday to acknowledge and honor the moment of his sacred parting from this earth, and all the spiritual and Holy moments spent with him during that hour on Friday, March 8th in the office of the Veterinarian. My Holy hour on this day is filled with tears once again, and longing for him and disbelief. It seems as if time stands still and we are ever together in two dimensions, and when I write of that hour today it is as if it is happening and nothing has happened since. We just *"are"* and *"every shall be,"* and nothing can separate us, not even earthly time. I believe at this writing that when I am finally with Rochester in Heaven that no time will have passed. We will be together once more and forevermore, and the pain of our physical separation will be wiped away. The price I pay now—the agony of not having him here physically—will be worth it all when we are reunited. I would far rather bear that suffering than my little one bear it, for he has done so much to help me through my life ever since he entered it. I would have given my very life for him, but perhaps living *without* his physical presence until we are together *is* my utter gift for him, to offer up for such an extraordinary priceless gift of himself he gave, and continues to give to me.

The holiest of all holidays are those
Kept by ourselves in silence and apart,
The secret anniversaries of the heart...
—Henry Wadsworth Longfellow

Mary in Our Lives

*Today people still fervently pray the Ave Maria all over the world—
collectively, fifty million times a day. Most of these hail Marys
are prayed as part of a rosary, a circular string of beads
that looks something like a jewel necklace
with a cross dangling off a little tail at one end.*

—Beverly Donofrio,
"Looking for Mary" or *"The Blessed Mother and Me"*

Saturday April 27, 2002

*I*T IS WRITTEN that the Rosary as we know it today, most historians trace back to the so-called Dark Ages of ninth century Ireland. Rosaries are divided into five decades (or sets of ten Hail Marys), separated by a single bead on which is said an Our Father and Glory Be. In my own personal history the Rosary became a part of my spiritual life in 1977. I taught myself, learning that to say a complete rosary I had to go around the circle three times, fingering the beads, praying, and meditating on one *"mystery"* per decade. The events of the lives of Jesus and Mary are called *"mysteries"* and begin with the Annunciation. The other events that follow are Christ's birth, death and resurrection. It all ends with Mary being crowned Queen of Heaven, the Coronation. There are 159 Hail Marys in a complete Rosary and these include the three said at the beginning of each circle for faith, hope and love. To pray once around the beads is enough, in common practice.

In February of 1977 it was then as a Protestant Methodist all of my life, that I began to pray the Rosary for my Dad who was having his larynx removed. Seeing him following his operation after hours of waiting and praying for him with my Mother in a Catholic hospital, is a memory that lives in my mind and heart and brings deep pain to this day. It is described well in one of my previous books. It was the Rosary I stumbled through praying as a novice in this new prayer form to help my Dad. I was using every prayer form I could think of, but this inexpensive turquoise blue rosary was a comfort to hold. That my Protestant Mother did not even comment that I was sitting there using one expresses well the dire and terrible situation.

Later in 1978 after my Dad's death in August 1977 and several weeks before my Mother's sudden death in September 1978, I placed this same Rosary into our open bottom step in our living room here in our cottage. It was part of a time capsule, and Bob and each of our children placed an object within this cavity. Bob then replaced and nailed shut the surface of the step, and shortly after the stairway was covered with carpet, and I became a Catholic in December of that same year. Putting the Rosary in the *stair step* signified this *step* into the Catholic Church I knew I was about to take. On the morning before the evening of my Mother's Church Service, her Memorial, our daughter Barbara gave me a most meaningful gift of a delicate pale blue Rosary to comfort me. I am still using it daily twenty-four years later. I also placed a small one decade Irish Rosary with shamrocks on each bead in my Irish Mother's hand as she lay in her casket before the Methodist service began. It was to tell her I was becoming Catholic. She had died before I could tell her.

Ten years later after Rochester came into my life I would fervently pray the Rosary for him when during a brief period of four to five days that seemed like an eternity I thought he was ill. This was due to a mistaken impression given to us by a veterinarian that Rochester was indeed seriously ill, and tests were done. I prayed in many ways for him described in two of my books, but it was at that frightening time I vowed to pray the Rosary daily for him from then on. I usually prayed the Rosary for him as he cuddled down on me. It was a form of prayer I felt led to do in gratitude to Our Lord and Blessed Mother for his complete health.

It is written—and I have shared it previously—that the baby Jesus was crying in His little manger in the stable and His Mother could not get

Him to sleep. One by one after each animal in the stable tried to calm Him to no avail, suddenly a little marmalade tabby cat jumped into the manger with the Christ child and gently lulled the Tiny One to sleep with his soft purring. How often Rochester has done that to himself and to me. The Blessed Mother Mary, ever so grateful, blessed the little cat and placed the mark of an "M" on the forehead of this tiny helper—and to this day, that breed of cat bears the "M" as a mark of Mary. My little Rochester, too, has an "M" on his forehead, and it is no wonder, therefore, that he was drawn to my Rosary Beads.

Often when in bed or in a chair praying my Rosary, if he was not already on my lap, he was drawn to come to me. It would touch my heart so deeply to see his tiny white paw reach out gently to pat the Rosary from time to time. He could not resist the beads and often would keep part of the strand immobile for a time, as he placed his paw on it and claimed it for his own.

All of these sharings that have seemed to spill forth here as I sit filled with memories, are to try to express what took place in the weeks before Chester left. Looking back on it as I have again and again in these past weeks, I have come to understand a portion of it all. But I believe there is more I am to know, and that I will. And I believe the knowledge I will be given will be comforting and help me to attain still yet another new dimension of living with Rochester, until we are together in Heaven.

Beginning in mid January or so of this year 2002, I began to have a much deeper desire to pray the Rosary and also what seemed to be a deeper love and need for Mary in my life. It became very intense and I believe it came about through reading a book about Mary I obtained in January. It spoke to me so deeply I read it three times in succession with no other reading during or in between. Before that I had read another new book twice (not about Mary but deeply spiritual) because I needed to fully absorb it. I see now how the two were spiritual messages for me strengthening and preparing me for the utter devastation to my soul and spirit in regard to Rochester.

But in these weeks before March 8th—I needed to pray the Rosary multiple times a day. It was as if needing a deep necessity like water. And when I would pray, Rochester was always with me on my lap in our writing room or lying facing me on my legs as I sat in bed at night. At night I would hold his paw as I prayed. He loved to give me his paws to hold.

And he would pat the Rosary from time to time and I was so happy with my precious little guy as we prayed I could never have imagined it was the light before the darkness. I just prayed and prayed and appreciated the role of Mary in our life (Chester's and mine) and how she was becoming more real and subtly prominent.

MARY'S ROSARY

On the chain the beads abound—
They circle 'round—and there is found,
A peace of heart in those who pray—
Our Blessed Mother's Beads each day.

The Rosary softly slips through fingers—
While on our souls her presence lingers.
As we lift daily our intentions,
She removes our apprehensions.

In moments still—this Chain of Love—
Links us to Mystical Rose above.
And as we pray the precious Beads—
Dear sweet Mary intercedes.

JGK

As a Protestant she was not prominently in my life or in the life of my family. She was thought about and portrayed in pageants at Christmas, and remembered at Easter as she stood at the foot of the cross where her son Jesus was crucified, but at other times she was not mentioned, or rarely. I had to come to know her more fully when I became Catholic. Even the Church I entered was named for her, "*Immaculate Conception*." Too, I chose the name of "*Mary*" as my confirmation name that night of December 13th. To begin to pray the Rosary in 1977 was strange, almost heretical due to my Protestant background, yet there are many Protestants that do pray the Rosary for I have come to know this through my reading. I only know one personally however, whom I have mentioned in a previous book and with whom I have exchanged correspondence and books.

A Protestant author writes in her book on Christian meditation that as a little girl her family had a little Catholic girl living with them and she and the girl shared a room. The author would notice how blissful the little girl was as she prayed her rosary each night and in stressful situations. She wished to have a rosary too but her Mother said they were only for Catholics.

This writer later found out you do not have to be a Catholic to use prayer beads and that people of all faiths who meditate use them. She herself bought inexpensive wooden beads and strung them and found they helped to keep attention focused on the inner words while fingering the beads as they pass through your fingers. She did not use them all the time. She states that the Rosary is a form of prayer opening the heart so that by the grace of God, we may receive the Holy Spirit.

Actually the word *beads* is derived from the Anglo-Saxon *bidden* (to pray) and *bede* (prayer) and are tactile reminders that we should bring prayer into our lives. I have read that two-thirds of the world's population pray with beads in daily life.

And so I believe beginning in January 2002 Mary was drawing me through this book I repeatedly read, and in turn through more frequent praying of her Rosary. Because she is so loving and wise, she knew I would need her more than ever when March 8th arrived, and so she gently drew me closer. And that is what I need to share this day for perhaps there are others who have kept her at a safe distance and refuse to allow her near, and maybe hearing how she has comforted me, she may be allowed to comfort you also. You do not have to be a Catholic or Protestant or any religion—you simply have to need consoling, comfort, and understanding, and love, and she will come to you. You do not even need a Rosary, for that is asking a lot of someone who may never have ever been near a Rosary before. I have just needed to share with you how Mary gradually entered my life since 1977, but then much much more so since January 2002. Having no earthly Mother for many years, or Dad, and feeling often like an orphan, it has helped me so very much to feel deeply Mary's love in a more apparent way. Her presence is here and comforting me as I live in this new dimension with my dear little Rochester.

And when I pray the Rosary, since I began with new fervor in January, after my reading, I pray for Rochester on the Rosary. It is totally untraditional but it is what I have been led to do. I do not pray the usual "*mysteries*," but pray the *mystery* I have been shown to pray with deep love and intensity, occasionally including Bob and myself, in a *"Hail Mary"* with Rochester (along with the Lord's Prayer and Glory Be). But basically I pray again and again for him, and I believe it is a chain and a link to God and Heaven through Mary that connects Rochester and myself for all eternity. It is not our only connection and communion of course, for I have told you of the others that are so incredible, but it is an unexpected one that began weeks before March 8th, and that I am drawn to repeatedly. And I know I will be shown the rest of the secret shortly in regard to Rochester, myself, the Rosary and Mary. The Protestant author too, that I mentioned previously, did not pray the Rosary in the traditional way but used a Logos of scripture with words of Jesus. A portion of words in the Hail Mary are from scripture also.

As I pray, I know with a certainty Chester's little white paw is on my one hand as he pats the Rosary with his other little white paw, and I cry and cry. Though I cannot see him he is always there, my little beloved.

The Rosary too is in my hand after praying it as I fall asleep, and Rochester's paws are still in my hand when I wake and I pray briefly anew. The Rosary goes with me around the cottage as does Chester. I have several Rosaries that mean much and I place them upstairs and down— one is even kept in a shoulder bag for when I go out. The beads remind me I am not alone. Mary and Chester are with me always—as is our Lord. When I complete this journal I am going to create for Rochester a special Rosary made of significant objects and beads and rocks. He will help me.

I write this on a Saturday—which in the Catholic Church is considered to be Mary's day. Praying Mary's Rosary with the repetitive words can often put you in a trancelike state which helps to be more receptive and open to God. It is peaceful—and comforting when prayed alone (with only Rochester), but I have never been able to pray it aloud with a group following Mass as is often done—never! For myself I need the quiet and my Rochester, and I pray it silently within myself.

And though I weep and weep, it is a strength emotionally and spiritually to know we two are together and praying, and that it will sustain me in all my days and nights along with my other forms of prayer, meditation, and Rochester's ever present presence.

Traditionally, prayer beads have consisted of strings of similar-sized beads, seeds, knots, or even rose petals and beads made from crushed roses, from which we get the word "rosary."

—Eleanor Wiley

The Rosary kept on my desk is made of crushed roses, and years after receiving it as a gift its lovely scent is still there. Rochester's white paws have caressed this one too.

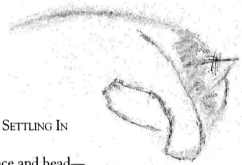

Settling In

Little furry face and head—
An inch from mine—I lie in bed.
He stares into my eyes and purrs
Then walks my body—he prefers—
To settle down on legs awhile,
Then moves to tummy—he knows I'll—

Not move an inch—he's here to stay
Because he knows now that we'll pray,
I with my Rosary—now the beads—
Know too, sweet paws and purrs and kneads.
In union with the breaths I take—
He's lulled to sleep until we wake.

Dedicated to Rochester—   JGK
companion in prayer
and all things of life.

Like a wreath of graces her Rosary she's given—
To her loving children as a key to heaven.

—unknown

Expect Nothing

Our grief may seem sometimes as if it were a real live animal thing that has taken hold of us. We have learned to make room for it inside ourselves, and it travels with us wherever we go.

—Unknown

Sunday, April 28, 2002

GRIEF, ESPECIALLY WHEN IT CONTINUES, simply is not understood by most. Lack of understanding by even our closest friends or family members may be surprising and extremely hurtful. This can be so in regard to both human and creature loss. Often a limit of time allowed for our grieving is put upon us though never truly expressed in words, or if they are they can be hurtful ones. If we talk to anyone at all or just a very select few we want that person or persons to know how we feel. Often we feel desperate within, and too we feel desperate inside when someone we thought we could count on simply seems to evaporate, or if they are occasionally available to talk but totally avoid the subject of our beloved one's death. This can create a loneliness, but for myself I would rather have that than superficial talk. Since our deadline for our grief to end is often laid down for us by others who seem not to understand at all, it is safer to confide in very few. Reducing our expectations makes the entire situation easier and does not waste our energy. Losing an animal companion is not understood by those who do not love animals or do not have an animal companion, and we have to recognize when there is insufficiency in a person's understanding and guard ourselves. It is better to not

98

be in the presence of such ones, whether in actuality or by telephone or correspondence.

To borrow a phrase of Bob's that has helped me through the years in situations I have had to face, is also comforting now. I even wrote a poem on the subject. Bob tells me to *"Expect Nothing."* While it may seem hard and lacking hope, it actually is very strengthening, and you do not set yourself up for heartache.

It is written: *"Loneliness is to endure the presence of one who does not understand."*

The last two stanzas of my four stanza poem may help also those in sorrow.

EXPECT NOTHING

Expect Nothing!
No expectations from other source—
For if you do you'll learn remorse.
Wear your sorrow like a cape.
Protect your soul from further rape.
Expect Nothing!
Nothing!

Expect Nothing!
In this garment most unique—
You will find just what you seek.
True contentment—with a sigh.
You let your expectations die.
Expect Nothing!
Nothing!
Nothing!

JGK
1993

Today again in the early afternoon Bob and I had our own private little worship service in memory of dear little Rochester. We do this each Sunday.

A Journal for Grieving and Honoring

He who has gone, so we but cherish
his memory, abides with us, more potent,
nay more present, than the living man.
— Antoine de Saint-Exupery

Monday, April 29, 2002

I WAS KEEPING JOURNALS before Rochester was born and came into my life, but from his arrival on he was on the pages of all my journals, and sometime literally. When he was a kitten in September 1986 I came to our cottage with just Rochester to make a week-long retreat. We still lived in Pennsylvania then and I had never stayed in the woods alone. He was a consolation and there in everything I did, adding enjoyment and comfort to my heart when I was sad. I had come to the woods to solve some difficult problems in my life. He was there to hold and to cuddle with when I was frightened by outside noises at night, and it gave me great joy to feed him and play with him and be totally in his company.

I would sit on the sofa with my books nearby and my journal on my lap, writing down moments from my retreat or thoughts and reflections, in an attempt to come through the problems and my inner pain and sadness, and Chester would jump up and sit squarely on the pages of my journal and look into my face. Pictures of him on that retreat are in my two earliest books and they are precious pictures. Since I preferred Chester there over any possible thing I could put on those pages, I always

100

let him stay. He was more likely to bring healing to me than anything else that found its way onto those blank sheets.

I have written about journals in all of my books and written in journals for years, but it is a most healing thing to do in regard to the passing of a precious animal companion. Writing this book is like keeping a journal for Rochester, and I have the lovely new journal (Forever) with the moons on written about in a previous entry that is for him and our life together.

A journal is extremely helpful at particularly sad times, when grief is overwhelming and your emotions are devastated anew. Write down those feelings and get them out on paper. Seeing them there in the written word is like having a part of yourself visible that you can analyze and comfort, and you may better understand the emotions within yourself. Keep your journal regularly—and always use it at very difficult times that come out of the blue.

Try to use a bound book, perhaps a color you associate with your animal, or particular flowers in the design that held meaning in your lives, or a design on the cover that is pleasing or significant, that only you understand. I have earlier explained why I chose the journal that I did for Rochester. If you use just scraps of paper to record your thoughts and memories, they can end up lost or separated. That is true of any form of journal keeping. It is much finer to have a bound book that is easily bought in a book or art store with a nice cover of your choice. Everything then will be in order and you will have it forever—the sad and the joyful—all of which were and are a part of you and your relationship with your beloved animal.

Your may use several journals filling one after another if you are inclined to write. I will do that. It is good! You can write poems in your journal for your friend. You can also write poems or quotations written by others in books or magazines that apply to your dear one—and you can copy them in, to be scattered amongst your own writings and feelings. To keep a journal is healing, and it is a private place to meet your precious animal in thought and prayer (you may compose written prayers for him or her) and through your personal writing about him that pours out from your soul. I know this will help you.

As I write this and many times when I write in Rochester's journal I am in tears. I can barely see. But the writing is a form of prayer and healing, though it may not seem to be at that time. You may wish to keep a second journal also, your own journal that you normally write in. Only you can decide as to whether to keep one or two at this time.

In your own journal, your survivor journal, you may use it to make sense of things, explore various facets of your life, or get rid of feelings that are difficult. Even if you enter them multiple times, each entry helps you one small bit. You can revisit the life you led with your loved one, just as you will in your special journal for your companion. Many men keep journals and especially when grieving. Men isolated in their grief have found they could unburden themselves by writing daily. Anyone can of any age. Through darkness and fear, guilt and confusion, and anger or frustration or any feeling one is experiencing, writing, more than any other activity can lead us through our emotions. Some may say conversation also is good, but that is often painful to me. When I am afraid of something or cannot face Rochester's absence at times, I write or meditate. I spend my days in the writing room that Rochester and I shared each day and his presence is forever here with me. My own written words will be my help in my grieving, for Rochester helps me write and we are one in God. I am creating a living treasure that will provide comfort to me through our written journal, and hopefully to others through this book. As I write I will think of my writing as a gift to my sweet beloved Rochester for having been in this world, and for loving me and inspiring me and being my faithful companion. I will think of my writing as a psalm and song of praise for him. I will honor him for as long as I live, my gift from God.

SPIRITUAL TREASURES

In a journal that I keep—
That helps me supernaturally leap—
The veil—to separate and hide—
I write his life—and still confide—
My poems, thoughts, and things of worth,
To his spirit here on earth.

For Rochester   JGK
                                                                 April 29, 2002

Longing

We long for the loved one to come back, to be alive in the world with us.
The death of our loved one, we feel, has diminished the world itself.
—Carol Staudacher

Tuesday, April 30, 2002

MY MIND IS WALLPAPERED WITH MEMORIES AND HAPPINESS, and days filled with love, and our presence to each other, and the joy this all brought to us. I believe that we are ennobled by what we love and Rochester ennobled me. I found a mystical grace through loving him so very much.

When he came into my life I had so many heartaches and problems, and he gave me more strength in my loving of him. It is why I made the Retreat written about in my previous entry, and his love and presence strengthened me on that retreat and always. I grew stronger through loving him and gained more courage. Loving him and he me, sustained us.

Rochester was and is an inspiring and blessed companion. He passed on to me riches of indescribable worth, and above all he gave me wonder and a love of being alive and sharing this life with him. Before he was sent to me I was in despair and wanted to die. I have written of this in my first book, *Higher Ground*, which was a result of that Retreat. But he came to me and I was invincible! It seemed like I could do anything I tried to do. He was and is an enormous and great soul in a beautiful and soft furred

103

marmalade and white body with luminous golden eyes that searched and read and knew my every thought, and my heart—then, now and forever. We are one soul in God. Oh, to have those moments, days, and years again from the time we first met and belonged to each other. Each day I learn a little more of living together with him in this new dimension, and I am grateful for being given this gift.

BEREAVED

I am bereaved
     for you who believed
        in me.
I have grieved
    and grieved.

You who weaved
    love
       into every second—
And beckoned
    me to grow—
You know
    I treasure you —

      I always knew
        you are my Angel.

For dear Rochester   JGK
                                 April 30, 2002

Sacred Space

Sacred space is a physical place where the divine or the supernatural
can be glimpsed or experienced, where we get in touch
with that which is larger than ourselves.

—Peg Streep

Wednesday, May 1, 2002

ROCHESTER HAS ALWAYS INSPIRED ME to do many things in life, and particularly to write. Books, journals, letters and poetry he continually led me to create. My beloved Rochester is also symbolic of the Divine as I have expressed in various ways within these pages, an Angel in fur, and God-given breath of life bestowed on me at a time when I needed both an Angel and true incentive to begin my life of writing. My Angel often lies on my desk (now in spirit, not in reality) beneath the Icon of Christ that I drew a number of years ago in 1992, and he is breathtakingly beautiful, his presence a blessing on myself and my writing, my goals and my dreams, all of which he is a part. A precious animal like Rochester with his love, warmth, and affection, who loves to be near you and petted, is a Holy presence where God can meet you and heal you, console you, and comfort.

In my grief I could totally give in and not accept the gift of his spirit upon my desk or anywhere that I am, but spirit is life and divinity, and Chester is everywhere I am, and I accept his gift of love everlasting and presence most real.

My desk is part altar and acknowledges the sacredness of the space my beloved Rochester and I inhabit daily—and always shall.

I share the gift of my writing room with Christ, Mother Mary, my Angels, and my Rochester, once visible Angel—now in spirit. I know when he is not on my desk or sitting in the window, he is ever by me on the bed that is next to my desk and on his own soft wildlife quilt, folded in quarters and covered in patches of deer, moose, bear and other creatures along with patches of color. It is upon this he literally sinks down into for his cat naps. His dear body's impression is still there and too his precious scent. I still kneel and pray and draw in his scent each evening after my day of writing, and my tears flow.

No, death does not mean the end to a relationship, it is the beginning of a new one that is so alive and extraordinary if we can allow ourselves, in and through our grief, to experience all we are being shown by our beloved one.

Eleven years ago on May 5th in 1991 I wrote this poem for Rochester and it seems so appropriate to conclude now this meditation of May 1st.

PURRING PAPERWEIGHT

What could be more beautiful than this—
Dear cat contemplating in silent bliss.
Upon my desk in unmoving pose.
So pure of heart—free of life's woes.

Profiled in window—backdrop of trees—
Wafting through screen—the gentle breeze—
Entices closing eyes to slowly raise
Upon blue lake in meditating gaze.

He nobly sits—so utterly trusting.
Because I love him—I am adjusting.
For on my papers he has been alighting—
Until he moves—I cease that writing.

I take my pencil and waste paper scrap—
And pen this poem on my lap.
Sweet honorable companion—eternal friend.
In your faithful presence—I choose to bend.

Dedicated to Rochester   JGK
then and now.   May 5, 1991

I have never forgotten this lovely afternoon with Chester, and it brought tears all through the years whenever I thought about it. That day I not only wrote this poem for him but took his picture as I did almost daily. It was so moving and beautiful, and it later became the cover for Rochester's and my book, *Journal of Love: Spiritual Communication with Animals Through Writing*, published in 2000. I never tire looking at it. Such precious memories.

Eight Weeks

HERE TO STAY

Each night and day
    you lie
        upon my legs or lap.
Your spirit's here to stay—
    you did not die!
        An unknown map
you used—
    and traveled back to me
        to keep me warm.
My little Muse—
    although I cannot see,
        I feel your precious form.

For my dear Rochester   JGK
Written in the early AM

Friday, May 3, 2002

ON THIS DAY THAT MARKS EIGHT WEEKS of our physical separation, I have an appointment with the ophthalmologist. The examination was excellent and I know that Rochester has helped me. Driving home we pass through the general area of the town of the Veterinarian's office, the place where I last held Rochester's dear little body. Bob treats us to dinner at one of our favorite restaurants on Route 16, the Miss Wakefield Diner. I glance at the clock and it is the very time Chester and I last embraced while he was on this earth physically. I do not wear a watch and Bob is hoping I will not see the clock, but we are sitting opposite it. A wave of despair washes over me again. It cracks open my heart and tears flow. I do not need a Friday or a clock to have it happen. My plate of vegetables sits untouched until I gather up all that just broke apart and fell invisibly all around me in the booth. Finally I am glued together with silent prayers for help and Bob's comforting words.

Words from
an Old Journal

*Let a man decide upon his favorite animal and make a study of it,
learning its innocent ways. Let him learn to understand its sounds
and motions. The animals want to communicate with man.*

—Brave Buffalo, *Teton Sioux Music (1919)*

Tuesday, May 7, 2002

I HAVE BEEN READING IN SOME OF MY OLDER JOURNALS because of
Rochester. Reading pages of love I have written about him through
the years is uplifting, yet moves me to tears. He gave me such courage and
made me strong. Because of his love and mine for him I was able to write
and do things I would have doubted myself on otherwise. When he came
into my life things were very difficult, and his companionship and love
strengthened me and changed me for the better.

In reference to the quotation that begins this day's entry, I also made
an entry about it in an older *"Angel"* journal where I had written the
entire quotation. That journal is a journal in which I recorded all things
about Angels and Angel encounters in my life, and about Rochester, for
he too was an Angel. The date is April 24, 1994 and I write—

*Though this subject is something I have prayed about since Rochester came
into my life—since February I have asked the Angels' help on this too. I
have always felt that if I gave myself to Chester and "listened" to his
communication to me that is soundless, but very real and evident, that we*

could enter into a very deep relationship, and that he too would deeply understand me because I was so open to him, and always striving for a deeper level with him. I believe we have achieved a very deep knowledge of each other and communication with each other, but it is on-going. It is something I work at every day and our life together is so precious. I feel closer to Chester than to other humans, except for Bob, because we work at this almost moment by moment. I wrote about this in Compassion for All Creatures *also, long before I read this quotation that just confirms all that I feel and have been experiencing with Chester.*

I went on to learn more about communicating with him and then we wrote the book *Journal of Love: Spiritual Communication with Animals Through Journal Writing.* I would never have imagined that when dear little Rochester came into my life that soon we would be able to communicate in a way far beyond what I have ever hoped or dreamed. It is a blessing that extends to the present when he is in spirit, and it shall last 'til we are reunited in Heaven. I write each message down now as always in our journal just as I did when he was here physically in body.

Other words said by Brave Buffalo in the complete quotation from which I have lifted words that begin this entry, and recorded by Frances Densmore are:

I have noticed in my life that all men have a liking for some special animal, tree, plant, or spot of earth. If men would pay more attention to these preferences and seek what is best to do in order to make themselves worthy of that toward which they are so attracted, they might have dreams that would purify their lives.

He also ends this quotation by saying that man must do the greater part in securing an understanding.

I am so grateful Rochester and I learned to communicate, and it is a gift we were blessed with while he was present in body and now continues. It is available for all those who wish this amazing and enriching connection with their beloved animals. Read about this and take the time to learn, and ask God's help. The Angels too will be there for you.

There is a wonderful quote in regard to animal communication that sums it up well:

Truth passes through three stages:
opposition, ridicule, and finally self evidence.

LISTENING!

Through the ether
    I receive your word
        and write it down.
            And though some
                may think it absurd—
I clasp it to my heart
    in appreciation—
        one word, then the next—
           and await in anticipation
              the full text.

For dear Rochester   JGK
                                      May, 2002

Rochester stretched out on our desk after a session of journal writing

Other Worldly Blessings

I fell asleep thinking of him,
And he came to me.
If I had known it was only a dream
I would never have awakened.

—Ono No Komachi (9th century)

Friday, May 10, 2002

ON THE EARLY MORNING before the sun comes up I am given a dream. It is of Chester. Each night before sleep and after my prayers I ask to be blessed with a dream of him, but it does not happen in all these weeks since March 8th. In fact, though I know I dream, I cannot remember any and am left with only fragments at times.

But this dream comes as a gift and it is so true to life that I cannot bear to learn it is a dream, and I crumble. Rochester and I go into the bedroom in the dream, and I shut the door. He jumps up and runs the length of the bed and onto the bookcase headboard. From there he steps onto the window sill at the open screened window to check out the night breezes, and moon, and sounds from the woods. All of this is what occurred in life night after night. Then as soon as I was comfortable he would settle down to sleep on my legs. He still does in spirit. I feel him there and his warmth. We hold hands and paws as he faces me extending his paws for this reason alone.

I see him there in the window, and suddenly there is a loud noise and I wake. The disappointment that it is not reality is so saddening, but that

113

I am given this dream causes me to thank Jesus, Mary and the Angels. The loud noise is a mystery, for all seems to be ordinary in our dark room. It must be a noise from my dream. At last my little one appears to me in a dream and I want to hold him forever! I feel comforted that he is exactly as when he was truly in our room, and that the dream was like a moment in true life.

Early in the morning I have a period of meditation as I do every morning there on the sofa with my back to the sliding glass doors for approximately twenty minutes. All the bird feeders above the deck are behind me, and Rochester, in spirit just as he always was in life, is on my lap. I go deeply in spirit into my meditation and sit motionless. When I slowly end this period I speak softly to Rochester from my heart and then slowly stand. As I turn to look outside I feel like I am seeing another world! Literally dozens of birds of every kind rise up and fly from the deck floor, the railing, the feeders! Never has there ever been such an enormous congregation of birds as this since we owned the cottage! It is surreal!

There is every bird that has been here this spring and more! I catch fleeting glimpses of Mallards, Woodpeckers, Starlings, Blue Jays, Chicka-dees, Nuthatches, Red Winged Black Birds, Baltimore Orioles, Mourn-ing Doves and dozens more! And yes, the Crows! Always my two Crows, though many more seem to join them from the grass. That I am even able to see and recognize so many in this moment caught in time, is outstand-ing. This is no mere incident nor was it any mere gathering. It is other-worldly and with great significance. I have that confirmed in my heart and soul. It has everything to do with Rochester. I feel in my spirit that they were gathered on the deck due to my deep prayer and meditation, and in ways known only to God they were drawn there through the passage of prayer, and to honor Chester. I also feel they were sent to comfort me, for only God could cause such an outpouring of wild life on one deck, all gathering behind me on the other side of the glass doors as I prayed and wept, and yet not make a sound as they normally do. I believe they were praying with me, visible signs of the supernatural, and power of prayer, and assurances of Rochester's presence. They were like a heavenly silent choir accompanying me, and when our prayer ended their voices were all freed and let loose as they flew in one giant flock! I will never forget this! I am so grateful.

Tears move heaven and are prayer
Behind the eyelids ready there—
To come to fullness to express
That which beyond words—they confess

JGK

Spending the day writing as always, I stop at 5 PM to again meditate for an hour because it is Friday, and within this hour Rochester passed. I sit silently in my writing room with him and meditate, pray the Rosary, and know that Chester upon my lap, is lightly patting the beads. Though I have had many tears, I was given blessings of Chester today most precious and powerful. Yes, I am so grateful for these gifts from another world and realm.

PRAYERS OF TEARS

Tears are prayer beads of us all
Arising often without call—
An overflowing from the heart,
Perhaps great joy will make them start.
Tears oft' rise from some deep sorrow—
Tears come today; they'll come tomorrow.

Expressions of the heart are good—
Tears happen naturally as they should.
Condemn not crying—feel no shame—
Moistened eyes pure love proclaim.

For my Rochester   JGK
pure love

Pennies from Heaven

Absence diminishes small loves and increases great ones,
as the wind blows out the candle and blows up the bonfire.
—La Rochefoucauld (Maxims)

Sunday, May 12, 2002

*I*T IS MOTHER'S DAY and we are headed up Route 16 to Center Ossipee to attend services with our daughter and son-in-law and three children at the First Congregational Church of Ossipee across from their Inn that they live in and run. Our son and daughter-in-law and three children are visiting at the Inn and we will all go to church together. We stop at the Rite Aid pharmacy on the way and Bob runs in to buy a Sunday paper. On the way out he finds a shiny penny on the sidewalk and presents it to me. He knows what I am thinking. I tell him it is a penny from Heaven, a gift from Rochester, and this simple coin is symbolic to me. The tears that are always on the edge come forth. On April 21, another Sunday, Bob found three pennies outside our local store when buying a paper that I have written about earlier. The smallest things have meaning for me because I believe there are hidden messages and my love is so deep. We hope to be in Heaven one day to be with Rochester forever. How significant that each penny is engraved with the words *"In God We Trust."* I am entrusting God with my beloved Rochester and our reunion.

116

EXPECTANT

Because I am expectant
the smallest thing
that happens
expresses
you.

For Rochester   JGK

Memory Loss

*Some memories are realities, and are better than anything
that can ever happen to one again.*

—Willa Cather

Monday, May 13, 2002

*W*HEN WE ARE GRIEVING we are not always as we were before. When
we have depression that occurs in grief in response to the death
of a person or beloved pet, it is stated in *The Memory Cure* by Thomas H.
Crook III, Ph.D., and Brenda Adderly, M.H.A., that this reactive depression decreases your ability to concentrate on outside matters. Therefore
it can also impair your memory. But as the process of mourning progresses
this type of memory problem usually lessens over time.

It is not completely clear why depression causes memory loss. It is
written that more than likely it is a result of the lowered motivation
experienced during depression rather than a fundamental breakdown. It
does not really seem too important to remember new information when
you are depressed and so sad.

I mention this now in our Journal for I have experienced frequent
times of memory loss since Rochester went to Heaven. Though I have
been writing every day since this occurred, and have been sharp concerning all I am writing, often when not engaged in writing my memory is less
than perfect. Usually the things I fail to remember are everyday practical
things, but also surprisingly there have been some matters of importance

that I would never have failed to remember before. It is true, other areas in life just are not as important to me now, and so I do not even try to remember something that previously I would have found necessary to retain, and done so without effort. In fact some things pass over me without my even thinking of them at all. I only know this through conversations with Bob or him calling attention to it.

Other symptoms of depression in addition to profound sadness or complete loss of interest in usual everyday activities include persistent fatigue, difficulty in decision making, loss of appetite, restlessness, feelings of inadequacy, insomnia, a desire to be more alone and thoughts about death or suicide.

Please take care of yourself if you are grieving and believe that your memory will improve gradually if there have been incidents of loss.

A man's real possession is his memory. In nothing else is he rich, in nothing else is he poor.

—Alexander Smith, nineteenth-century Scottish poet

The Floral Tin

All profound things and emotions of things
are preceded and attended by Silence.

—Herman Melville

Tuesday, May 14, 2002

I have not opened yet the lid of the floral tin.
I am not yet strong enough to look within.

JGK

BEING QUIET IS THE PATH I CHOOSE TO EXPERIENCE MY GRIEF. Chester and I were always quiet and loved being together in silence with only the sounds of nature floating through our windows. Therefore I could not possibly want otherwise now for I choose to be as I was with him always. Silence helps me to be more at peace, though I am grieving. Silence is a restorative place within myself also, where I live in privacy with Rochester. It is difficult to be amongst a lot of talk or noise. Bob is a quiet person also and we do not need a lot of conversation when we are together. We are both reflective, and find quietness conducive to thinking, reading, and to even inspiring more interesting conversations when we do talk.

And so to spend my time alone all day in writing and prayer, is what I need and always did with Rochester. It is only natural I would remain the same as I live with his spiritual presence.

I also live in the presence of his ashes that are inside the brightly colored floral tin. This container has been more comforting than I could have imagined. I never get over its significance, yet seeing it often overwhelms me and leaves me bereft. Other times it is extremely consoling. I know without a doubt cremation was the right decision. That decision helped keep me sane. But I am so fully aware of his presence with me in spirit, that the floral tin is often shocking to me when it strikes me anew of the contents.

When I first brought his ashes home I thought I would place the container in one place. That thought was swept away from the first night. A sentence from the entry I wrote of March 20th when I brought his ashes home has proven to be true. I wrote: *"this tin will be my silent companion forever."* It travels within this small cottage daily and does not have a permanent home—except this cottage itself. It does not sit on a shelf or desk but goes where Chester was when he was in body. During the day I place it next to Chester's wildlife comforter on the bed in our writing room. I do not place it in the comforter for I know with all my being that his spirit being is lying in that comforter just as he did in body. I also place his purple collar with tags on the one corner of the comforter and a velveteen green pouch that holds his fur we had trimmed from him on another. The fur is in a small plastic bag within. Later I may encase small portions of it (but not all) with his picture into several prayer cards or Holy cards I may create and laminate after I complete writing this book. At least they are my thoughts now. I may change. I am changing even now as I write. Often when we write, things surface to change us. There are many little remembrances I will do later, though I continually create them even while writing this book. Always his red collar remains upon my left arm. That is forever.

At night the tin sits on the sofa with me as I read or watch television with my legs stretched down the length as I did for almost 16 years. I know with a certainty his spirit lies upon the bathrobe that is on my legs, though the tin sits next to us. It is the same when I sleep, the bathrobe upon me and his spirit upon the robe and the tin on a table next to the bed. All these rituals, if that is what can be said of them, may seem strange to some, but I know they are far from strange to others. Many have had and will have rituals with their own beloved animal and human companions, and grieve for them deeply. Many find rituals are necessary in grieving just as they were in the years of joy of living, when their companions were ever with them and in sight day and night. Taking away the rituals and objects and belongings that were part of any love and deep relationship be it human or animal companion, is an individual decision. Each person is different, each relationship is different. No one can tell anyone else what to do, or when, or if to do it at all.

When I opened my Steno pad I carry around, under April 26th (though I do not always date things in these pads like I do in my journals) were the words beneath the date that opens this entry. I had not realized the hurried words I entered were a little poem. And now some weeks later I still have not looked within the floral tin. The lid is still taped shut on two sides as I received it. I do not know when or if I will ever be ready to remove the lid.

SACROSANCT

Just as my earthly body
      is a receptacle for your Anima
         and heart—
This flowered tin
      protects and holds
         your earthly remains.

Each enfolds
      your precious being—

         each ordains
            your presence
              Sacrosanct.

For Rochester   JGK
—Sacrosanct—   May 2002

Making a Connection

And dreams in their development have breath,
And tears and torture and a touch of joy.

—Lord Byron

Wednesday, May 15, 2002

T IS WRITTEN that many of the messages we receive in dreams are connected with the hopes, concerns and anxieties of everyday life. Though most of my dreams are difficult in the sense of finding true messages, I am grateful for the first dream I had of Rochester of May 10th. It was not surreal but very real, and was like a movie taken of our night time ritual. It indeed dealt with everyday life.

Last night I was again blessed with a dream of Rochester that was a typical several moments captured from the past, with one exception.

Chester is lying on his right side on the green carpet in the small area outside our writing room at the top of the stairs. He is waiting for me at the end of our writing day. I check something on my desk in relation to my new book (I see the title on the paper), and then pick Chester up with great affection and hold him horizontally in my arms. As I watch, he starts to disappear beginning with his head, until he is invisible. The dream ends.

I wake up suddenly and my first reaction in this strange state is that I am overjoyed. I feel again it is confirmation of his presence always in the everyday living of our continued life together. That I wake with this

123

feeling of assurance and joy is a gift, as well as the vivid dream itself. I know this dream, and the one before, are messages from Rochester and Heaven, and that he is truly here in spirit. I do not need a dream to tell me, but the fact that two have done so, and so clearly, is incredible. I record it at once as I am doing here. I am extremely grateful.

> *The world is not conclusion;*
> *A sequel stands beyond,*
> *Invisible as music*
> *But positive as sound.*
>
> —Emily Dickinson

Rochester awaits me there, while continually affirming his spirit presence with me always.

Ten Weeks

Why oh why . . .
Do they call it GOOD-bye?
          —from a greeting card designed by C. Bainton

Friday, May 17, 2002

I KNEW

With eyes closed
          and head bowed—
I stood alone
          amongst the flowers.
Racks of potted plants
          all about—
Tears streaming
          down my cheeks—
My heart convulsing
          with grief.

Having rushed
          from the store
Hoping not
          to be seen—
Now hidden behind
          a shelf of blossoms,

125

I relived in pain
        that hour—
Still present—
        as on that day,

No one knew
        I stood and wept alone
Except my little
        beloved—
Who is ever present
        and in my heart.

When this long period
        passed
And I opened
        my eyes—
Through falling tears
        I saw a ball of color
                at my feet—

The only bloom
        upon the ground
                lay by my shoe.
And as I picked it up
        and kissed it—
                I knew.

Written for my   JGK
little beloved Rochester   May 2002

It is only the third time I have to be away from home on a Friday and all three in the period of 5 PM. Each time we are required to be out we are forced to be near to the Veterinarian's clinic. Today it is to pick up glasses for the two us at the optician's office. When finished there I walk quickly into the adjoining Wal-Mart store to look at a certain book before going to our car. Instead, as I walk down an aisle I look at my watch. I have been hoping to beat the clock as we arrive at the optician's. Seeing the hands of my watch at a minute after five I dissolve into tears and fall apart. I actually feel weak and go amongst some clothing racks alone until I am secure. Then walking quickly back out through the store crying all the way with my head down trying to be unnoticeable, I rush out the door and into the rows of floral displays. On the sidewalk I find a hidden place behind the shelves containing large flowering plants and lean there against a soda machine. I cannot stop sobbing and just remain immobile for a long period. I do not care if I am seen. I do not know. My heart is breaking as if for the first time. When my emotions begin to subside, my head already bowed, I open my eyes to see through the blur, a blotch of color touching my black sandal.

I pick up the ball, a flowering ball! Most sections of it still are in many buds, the rest with three or four bright pink blooms. I know immediately without one moment's hesitation of thought, that this lovely bright flower with its endless possibilities of new bursts of pink, is sent to me by Rochester in my despair. He can never stand to see me cry or be ill in any way. He always comes onto my lap to comfort me and pat my hands with his dear white paws. Then he remains hours if needed.

This day he sends a bright pink ball of color to cheer me and one with buds that will continue to flower and bring me solace. He knows I will know it is from him. We always know such secrets about each other.

Twenty minutes pass there behind the shelves of plants as I keep my tear filled vigil of his passing ten weeks previous. All the plants displayed are large, and many huge ones standing in groups. No small plants are present from which this flowering ball can drop. No other flowers or greens lay in the aisles. Only that flower that Rochester left by my shoe. I share it all with Bob as he comes out of the store looking for me. At home I place the flowering gift on Rochester's table in a clear small bowl of water to float, a clear bowl identical to the one containing Rochester's water.

If only we believe and do not doubt the impossible, we receive the unimaginable to nourish our broken hearts. But we must not doubt.

O no, we did not want to say "GOOD-bye."
We were forced to say "SAD-bye."

If I had a single flower for every time I think about you,
I could walk forever in my garden.

—Claudia Grandi

Sacramental

ANGEL

For you who believed
    in me
        I am bereaved.
I have grieved
    and grieved.
O how you weaved
    your love
        into every second—
And beckoned
    me to grow.
You know
    I treasure you—
        and always knew
            you are an Angel.

For Rochester   JGK
                                                      2002

Sunday, May 19, 2002

I BELIEVE THAT OUR ASSOCIATION with animals, birds and other creatures is essential to us and our holiness. We must not treat them as less. It is written that St. Francis's association with animals

128

caused him to speak of them as his brothers and sisters in the great universal family. He came to the realization that the relationship was not that of being inferior to the supposedly superior, but rather that of brotherhood and sisterhood.

Animals can be an essential part of our pilgrimage to God. I know Rochester has drawn me and continues to draw me closer to God than any human ever has. He was and is an Angel, but just in my daily living with him he brought so many blessings and gifts and attributes into my life. He brought out my noble nature, though it could not be compared to the noble nature of his own. He was and is my companion and teacher for I was drawn to learn and write about subjects I might never have turned to or investigated had he not entered my life. My almost sixteen years spent with him were enriched and blessed, and filled with mysteries and discoveries, including learning to more deeply communicate with each other in wondrous ways. Friendship and companionship and love are among our best teachers. He gave me these, and together we were fantastic. He put a life in me that was pure delight because he loved me and taught me things and longed to be with me—and I felt I could do things I never did before because I loved him so and we belonged to each other. He was a sacramental, beloved and cherished, and ever shall be.

SACRAMENTAL

He lies serenely upon the bed—
Soft white paws extend forward in beauty and grace.
The sun streams in upon his head
And closed eyes, warming and transforming his precious face
And presence—in these moments of deep contemplation.
I look upon this golden creature bathed in light—
Soul of my soul—a jewel of God's creation—
And see the Angel that keeps my heart bright.

For Rochester   JGK
with my love   February 28, 1997

Food for
Thought and Spirit

Setting the table is a hearth ritual, and there are no rules.
It is a symbolic act that assists you in infusing daily life with soul.
It's sacred time, even if it is just for one person.
Don't fret if your intention isn't clear.
Just by making the space to listen,
you will, in time, hear what wants to be heard.

—Anne Scott,
Serving Fire: Food for Thought, Body, and Soul

Tuesday, May 21, 2002

ROCHESTER HAS ALWAYS HAD A FINE FEEDING TABLE here in New Hampshire. He never ate from dishes on the floor. A former maple record cabinet with two louvered front doors and 22"x23"x23", the size of a night table, was his place for eating. It stands against a small kitchen wall and holds his plate for food and small bowl for water. He never drank much water. His plates are white china and of varied floral designs that I bought him from time to time in Maine, where prices were right and selections many. He ate his moist cat food fortified with supplementary vitamins from them. Eating from this table was not only rather lovely, but because of visiting family dogs it also kept his food safe from the smaller ones. When his two larger "cousins" were here I had to put his food plate way up out of reach for they often devoured his food in one lick. I would give food to Rochester at intervals then, and stand guard. He was never a big eater and never ate all of his meal at one time.

This little maple table that once held records in Pennsylvania, held photo albums after its move to New Hampshire in the late 80s, and served for Chester's dining. It was also where I kept his small stash of catnip which was an occasional treat. When Rochester was a kitten Bob made him a rugged scratching post from scratch and it is pictured with Rochester in my book, *Compassion for All Creatures*. He enjoyed this post and could both scratch on it and keep his nails trimmed down, and also sit on the top of it and watch the birds through the window. It had great rope cords in loops dangling too that he loved to swing on and bat around. I would on occasion rub catnip into the carpet covering (Bob put the carpet on wrong side out to make it tougher) and Chester would lick some and then roll around, and race around, and enjoy himself. Then he would be sedate again like it never happened. But every time I opened the cabinet doors his little head would be in there and his paw reaching for the cat nip box.

I always put down a pretty paper towel on the white marble top Bob had added to the wood of the cabinet. More recently in months past it was always a design in pink and blue of stars and moons. Rochester and I love the stars and moon. I place his bowls on the towel and along the back wall is a small vase of artificial African violets and a slightly larger vase with assorted flowers. Small blue and white statues of an Angel and Mary are under the flowers. Often Chester would sit on the table and wait for his meal if particularly hungry or I was not quite prompt enough. I was then helpless to do nothing more until I fed him. How could I resist?

Above the vases of flowers hangs a picture I took of Rochester that has had great meaning for me through the years. It is a tender picture as he is tender. He is ten months old and it is February 1987. He is sitting on our blue kitchen table in our former home in Pennsylvania next to a beautiful bouquet of assorted flowers. We had had them on the altar at the Methodist Church that morning in remembrance of Bob's father's birthday who had died five years previous to that. Now at home Rochester just wanted to sit by the flowers that Sunday. And so I took several sweet pictures of him that day and this one especially has remained in view through the years. It is in a 5x7 dark mahogany curved frame that highlights the pastels of the flowers and Rochester's beautiful coloring.

Nearby Rochester's table at the kitchen window I have a small altar. Several years ago I asked Bob to extend and widen our sill with a nice stained board, and I placed meaningful objects upon this creating a worshipful place to be when one was at the sink or counter working. There is a picture of it in a previous book of mine. One object it holds is a statue of St. Francis of Assisi who loved animals so, and several birds' nests I found, and other treasures spiritual relating to nature and Rochester, and an image of Christ, and a small statue of Mary. Now I have added a small photo of Rochester in a gold frame, the same photo that appears on his announcement I sent out following his entrance into Heaven, and a more recent one taken several weeks before he left framed in a wider frame of gold wood. He is sitting on his shelf on the screened in porch looking at me in love. He looks like a kitten. This very picture appears elsewhere in this journal.

Rochester's table now has become an altar also specifically for him. There is even a small pile of plastic milk bottle circlets from the lids in various colors that were his favorite toys. He would toss and spin them all around the rooms. I keep adding to his colorful pile of circlets out of habit as they lay in front of the blue and white Angel at the back of the table.

I know in other countries altars are common in kitchens and often real food like rice is put in bowls at these places of worship, or fruit placed there and incense burning. It is said sometimes entire meals were placed on these altars before statues of Buddha or others that were being worshipped, with fresh flowers. Today I add some fresh flowers too—not in worship, but in deep and loving remembrance . How long will I continue to place out one of Rochester's china plates and put five little pieces of tasty Iams food upon it? This dry food was used only as a treat for him and not daily, and only a few little morsels. He would love it when I got the orange bag out. Next to his plate of five Iams tiny morsels is his filled water bowl. I replace the water and food morning and night and use a different saucer, just as if he were here in reality. It is a sacred place and the filled bowl and five pieces of Iams are to signify that I know he is here as always, and they are there to show love to his spirit that is ever present. As I work in our tiny kitchen I feel him there, his presence almost tingling as he sits on his table.

His feeding always seemed to have significance. For most of his life he ate Friskies moist cat food fortified with the vitamins I spoke of earlier, then later he also ate moist Iams canned food. Ever since he was a kitten I loved him so much that I could not even throw away the sweet pictures of the cats' faces that appeared on the Friskies labels. I would remove each Friskies label and cut off the picture of the cat. I have a special container for them in my writing room. I decorated envelopes and letters with them, and corners of my journal pages through the years. Each picture is a lovely miniature work of art I could not destroy because of my great love for Chester. I have written in detail about this to honor Chester in my book, *The Enchantment of Writing*. I have enough of them stored to last a lifetime to use in remembrance of him.

When will I stop this practice of offering refreshment? I simply do not know. Placing his food before him and keeping his table attractive was always such a joy for me and he enjoyed that little table very much. He often sat there even when he was not eating. And certainly I could sense him there when I knew it was time to place his food before him. I still feel him there! This little ritual continually feeds his spirit now and not his tummy, and conveys to him my constant love even in the everyday things of life that we partake of together, and always will.

With respect to ritual, it must be kept alive.

—Joseph Campbell

AGAIN AND AGAIN

Upon your table
      a plate of white—
Is set for you
      each day and night.
With tokens of food
      For your dear spirit—
Your unseen presence
      does endear it.

Cool water too—
      for one I treasure—
That you may enjoy—
      at your own pleasure.
A fresh bloom today
      all budded and pink—

To tell you my love
     when you come for a drink.

Above your table
     a framed picture of you—
Is a feast for my eyes
     where you once feasted too.
Oft times we need symbols
     to ease the pain—
So I set your table
     again and again.

For my beloved   JGK
Rochester   May 2002

Icon of Love

Icons are special images that are considered "windows into heaven."

—unknown

Thursday, May 23, 2002

SOME MONTHS AGO when Barbara came to visit for ten days or so, she brought two unique hand made gifts created by her husband, our son-in-law, Francis. Both were inspirational, significant, and personal, but one I choose to write about now and share. It is a wooden image of Rochester, cut and hand painted by Francis, and made to look as close to Rochester in appearance that would seem possible. Not having Chester there to use as a model, Frank used the image of Rochester that appears in glorious color on the cover of my book *Compassion for All Creatures,* a picture that just melts me. Daily I look into those golden eyes and experience him looking into my soul, just as do his eyes in the picture I took that we used on the announcement sent out about Rochester's entering Heaven.

Just Rochester's beautiful face close up and his shoulders are on the cover of my book, but within on a page near the front is the same picture in full length and in black and white, taken by Francis. I used this picture along with all my personal photos I took of him for my book. Like the picture of him in color with the flowers I have written about taken in Jenkintown, Pennsylvania that hangs above his dining table, in the black and white picture inside *Compassion,* he is sitting again on our kitchen table, only it is our table in New Hampshire. Next to him in the picture sits a foam rubber holder for a can of soda that Frank placed there that reads *"I love N.H."* Instead of the word *"love"* is a red heart. Yes, Rochester does love New Hampshire.

The wooden image of him (11 inches by 6 inches) sits in our living room just below the precious painting mentioned previously that Barbara painted. They look beautiful as the focal points at the end of the room. The cut out image is so like Rochester I often pick it up and give it a kiss and a long hug. He sits and stares at me lovingly as I sit on the sofa in the evening and where I always sat with him and still he is there, stretched up my legs.

I am grateful to have this very life like and life-sized image, and this week came to realize how very true to life it must be. We are caring for four animal companions of our daughter Jessica, and husband Michael and children for eleven days. Both dogs, large and small, did double takes, barked and backed away thinking the image really was a cat. Yet the larger of the dogs had seen it often before.

Many family dogs of all sizes and personalities have visited and been taken care of here on little vacations, also two sweet bunnies, and even a very young pot bellied pig. Rochester had no trouble showing dogs of all sizes by his quiet and confidant demeanor that this was his home, but that little Vietnamese potbellied pig really frightened him.

But now—his handsome little wooden image can even stand his own ground no matter who the visitor! I am so thankful for it. Like the painting of him, it too is an icon of great spiritual wealth—a *"window into heaven"* as I look through it and pray.

IRRESISTIBLE

Your loving image sitting there—
Draws me to stare and deepening prayer.
Before I know it, I embrace—
Your precious form, and kiss your face.

For Rochester   JGK
                                                             May 23, 2002

An Invisible Cord

Write hard and clear about what hurts.
—Ernest Hemingway

Friday, May 24, 2002

STRANGE THINGS HAPPEN TO US WHEN WE GRIEVE. We are not as we were and may never be again. We are in another world. Some things just disappear from our memory, and others stay in seclusion until we are ready to remember, or strong enough for the hidden truths to emerge.

Often we cannot recall conversations or people, or even incidents that occur. Perhaps it is because there is a new entity in our life and its name is *"grief."* It is mysterious. Grief does really strange things to our memory.

At 5 PM I stop my writing of this book because slowly the aura of 5 PM March 8th comes upon me and the remembering too of the preceding day and hours. Tears drip down onto my paper and I set it aside and sit in my comfortable chair in my writing room away from my desk. It is in this chair I held Rochester so many times and still now too in spirit. I cannot bear this hour, and my tears and grief are so overwhelming I pick up my Rosary from the table and begin to pray. Knowing Chester has come onto my lap from his quilt quite near us on the bed, I begin the Hail Marys for him. Again and again I go around the Rosary, the concentration on the prayers and the fingering of the beads keeping me sane. At times I hear myself saying the prayers aloud so as to drown out my pain and sadness and to not fall apart. Again and again, around and around the beads in prayer saying my little one's name in the prayers, and including myself with him at times too, when a wave of despair seems to drown me. We sit there for an hour. At one point I open my eyes to look at the small clock across from me on the desk and it is at 5:12 PM. I envision all that has and is transpiring and pray louder. Then I ride the waves, and as if Mary has whispered in my ear to end my prayers, I conclude them. I open my eyes to see it is 5:57 PM. I have made it through the hour with my Rochester, and the Blessed Mother enfolding us in her arms. It does not matter that weeks have passed. The grief is ever new and fresh because we love so deeply.

Before sleep this night, and contemplating my earlier 5 PM vigil, a poem begins to form speaking of the grief that is ever present. I hurriedly scribble it in the dark.

UNVANQUISHABLE

Grief cannot
be forced to leave,
In loving deeply—
deeply we grieve.
We live in sorrow
and in anguish—
It's not an entity
we can vanquish.

For dear Rochester

JGK
May 24, 2002

Dreams may be the clearest passage to our corridor to eternity. I have read more than once that those we have loved who have gone before us are connected to us eternally as if by an invisible cord. In our past and our future and our absence and our presence and in our dreams, we are joined. Rochester and I are eternally one.

Night Visitor

And when he paused and hesitated
I felt the silence punctuated —

—JGK

Saturday, May 25, 2002

HE CONCLUSION TO THE DAY comes in a comforting way. That night in sleep I am given a third dream about Rochester. I am sitting in the striped chair in our living room near his painting and wooden images I have written about, and Rochester is lying on the top of the television very close by (about three feet away), and facing me, and just staring at me with love. I awaken immediately regretting that I have. He loved being on that television that was level with the window sill he sat upon, to view the large side yard of green grass, the birds, and woods behind and beyond.

Perhaps I long so for dreams like this that I try to snatch them up quickly so they will not disappear from my memory as most dreams do. I awaken peacefully, then tears fall and fall. I am so thankful for this dream! In the dark by night light only, I write it down in the steno pad beside my bed. As I try to fall asleep, Chester's presence felt deeply on my legs, I say prayers of gratitude for this dream so true to life, for it has happened many times in real life throughout our lifetime together, this very scene! No other dreams come but this one, and like the first two of them, is an assurance of his presence.

In the morning I am blessed again and anew by the dream. It reminds me of a dream I had about my Dad long ago and captured in a poem. Upon finding the poem that has much love woven into it and is six stanzas, I see small segments of it that apply to my visitation from Rochester. I copy them out to be placed into this entry with Chester's name replacing my father's. I believe that will please my Dad to share his poem with Chester, for it is he that I have asked to care for Chester until he and I are together in Heaven, as well as Blessed Mother Mary. I am so grateful for this life-like dream of Rochester.

NIGHT VISITOR

I saw my Chester in a dream—
Defined and clear, it did not seem—
This was a passing in the night—
Another world; it was delight—
To find him there again with me—
In moment I could not foresee.

For I know now my Chester came—
As handsome image—to proclaim—

I live! And though this is a dream—
You'll not forget my eyes—this gleam!
Forevermore—a veil away—
I walk with you through every day.
And even if your dream grows dim—
Trust and believe I live with Him!

For beloved Rochester   JGK
adapted from a poem   May 25, 2002
 originally for my Dad
written March 14, 1991

How other worldly that I had this dream of my Dad in March, a few days after the date of Rochester entering Heaven March 8th, 2002, to join him.

Reflection on Dreams

Between the two, we come and go—
—John Squadra, The Compass of the Rose

Sunday, May 26, 2002

There is the dream journey and the actual life. The two seem to touch now
and then, and perhaps when men lived less complicated and distracted
lives the two were not separate at all, but continually one thing. I have read
somewhere that this was once true for Yuma Indians who lived along the
Colorado River. They dreamed at will, and moved without effort from
waking into dreaming life; life and dream were bound together. And in this
must be a kind of radiance, a very old and deep assurance that life has
continuity and meaning, that things are somehow in place. It is the journey
resolved into one endless present.

—John Haines, *Moments and Journeys*

MY PRECIOUS DREAM OF LAST NIGHt and my reflection upon it remind
me of this meaningful quotation above I had entered in a
Journal, and now wish to enter here in Rochester's Journal. I say "amen"
to it. It speaks of how I am living life since March 8th, in *"one endless*
present." The quotation appeared in an inspiring issue of *Heron Dance: A*
Search for Meaning, for Beauty, a lovely publication from Vermont I often
read with Rochester on my lap.

Rochester's Room

ROOM OF TEARS

In this room filled with tears
Where we spent days and years—
Loving together—and writing—
A plaque now is citing
Your name and this place,
Where I looked upon your face.

In remembrance and emotion—
And undying devotion—
On the door it appears—
In this room filled with tears.

For sweet Rochester

JGK
May, 2002

Monday, May 27, 2002

ON THE DAYS AND YEARS Rochester and I spent together loving and living, we spent the majority of the hours in the front upstairs bedroom that overlooks the lake, and front gardens and lawn, and the prayer chair on the platform by the water. It was a guest room at times but always it was and is our writing room. I would write at my large desk under the front window with a view of all this beauty, but to my left on the folded wildlife quilt on the bed was the dearest beauty of all. Rochester. Every hour spent in his company I cherished, and he affectionately and lovingly stayed with me in the quilt, on the bed, or on my desk and papers. And too, on my lap. This room was filled with joy because of his presence. I could write and write with his angelic presence ever near inspiring me.

Today in the mail a handsome plaque arrives that Bob ordered for me. He had created its message for my approval and after discussion I changed only one word—*"spirit to presence."* It is 4" x 8" and brass-like in finish, with black engraving. I cherish this memorial, but still have great difficulty in accepting that it is needed. We go upstairs together and after choosing the place on the door of the writing room, Bob hangs the plaque.

It reads:

ROCHESTER'S ROOM

This Room Is Dedicated
To The Memory
Of His Sweet Presence

It hangs above a wooden angel all violet in color, holding a bouquet of straw flowers. She has been there several years and she and Rochester are acquainted. She is symbolic of the Angels who are in the room, including Rochester. Below her hangs a puffy violet or lavender star approximately eight inches wide and trimmed in gold. This always indicated that it was and is a *Star's room*, and always shall be. *Rochester's Room*.

Rochester's Birthday

OUR MUTUAL GIFT

On your birthday
      the coral Hibiscus blooms—
Not one blossom
      but three!
Reminding me
      of a trinity
I have realized you
      to be.

The Hibiscus
      planted for you that I cherish—
Too, in spirit—and nature's way,
      shall daily nourish
Each moment I am near it,
      my heart—
          and soul—
             and spirit.
Each blossom silently whispers your name—

Rochester

For dear Rochester
on his birthday

JGK
May 30, 2002

144

Thursday, May 30, 2002

*I*T IS YOUR SIXTEENTH BIRTHDAY yet you still looked like a very young cat. You never aged and never shall. It is your first birthday we have ever been apart physically. I think back on all the others and how we spent each one together. Your presents were light little toys you liked to bat around, a small orange bag of Iams cat food to be used a tiny portion at a time as treats, milk bottle circlets of various colors I would save up so as to have many on that day all a once, instead of just the ones pulled off regularly and tossed on the floor for you. How you loved to toss and chase them. And an empty bag all puffed up for you on the floor. You would dash into as if chasing something (and especially if I tossed a circlet into it first) and roll all around in the bag. That was a treat too, anytime after we had grocery shopped. Also, a carton for your birthday to investigate and hide in—all yours! I have so many pictures of you in cartons, just your sweet face peeking out. Simple things you liked. And always a container of grass grown just for you, bright and green to nibble on. It was even worthy of a poem I wrote just for you. Yes, always there were poems written for your birthday (or any day) and I give you two today. Such sad words they are, not happy poems like the past. But I cannot write now what I wrote in the past. I can barely read the poems of the past. But still I need to write your poems.

You had other gifts too, and often a new collar. So many pictures I would take of you, but not only on your special day. Every day here together was special.

Today I walk outside in the morning to find three coral blooms wide open on the new Hibiscus we planted for your birthday. They are soft and brilliant and I take pictures of them for our journal. Also I take the wooden image of you from the living room and carry it out to your Hibiscus and sit it under all the dark green foliage. I take more pictures. The purple Rhododendron planted for your birthday are blooming too. Everything here where you lived and still reside, celebrates you, little one. I carry your wooden image indoors. So many little rituals I do throughout the day that only we two did together. And too, I pray, and especially the Rosary for you. And I sit and stare and cry too. I have tried my best not to make this day sad, filling it with joyful memories of our years together. But the tears always come.

But it has been a precious day because it is yours and Janna's. That is how our life together began, with and because of Janna. How grateful I am for you, for Janna, and that day of June 23rd in 1986.

It has been a Holy day for me, and I write you another poem. Though it is sad, it ends with the knowledge of certainty that we shall be together forever. Happy birthday, dear Chester. You made my life like a birthday every day.

How?

How can I spend your birthday
    without you?
Without your soft marmalade fur,
    your golden eyes—
Your gentle, soothing purr
    your soft white paws—
Your precious body
    everywhere I am.

I surmise
    I shall survive.

Higher laws
    leave me bereft—
        your absence gnaws
           my shattered heart.

In a dimension of our own
    we live—
        until that day.

For sweet Rochester   JGK
May 30, 2002

Rochester with
Iams bag and grass

Wooden image of
Rochester with his
Hibiscus plant

By Rochester's life
and his being with us—
our lives were enhanced.
When he died
our lives were diminished.
But the enhancement
of his presence
was so much
greater
than the diminishment
of his passing.

Bob Kolb
May 30, 2002
Rochester's 16th birthday

The Vigil

Be not forgetful to entertain strangers:
for thereby some have entertained angels unawares.

—Hebrews 13:2

Friday morning, May 31, 2002

IT HAS BEEN TWELVE WEEKS TODAY that Rochester left me physically. It seems like yesterday. It is impossible for me to believe that this time has passed. The pain has never left me or diminished, the tears are ever present. But I embrace it all, as I do Rochester in spirit continuously.

On Thursday, March 7 when we learned the tragic news from the Veterinarian and went back to the office to take Rochester home again with us, he just lay there in his carrier. His little paws held my hand and he rested his head on them and lay motionless. I said soothing words to him while I sat frozen and locked in fear. I could not bear to lose him. I wanted to scream. Once home and taken out of his carrier he immediately ran upstairs to our writing room. For a few moments he hid under one of our white chests there and then slowly came out to me.

I held him on my lap and soothed him and embraced him and whispered love words to him only we share. How could I ever let him leave me? It was unbearable to think about.

A bowl of water on a paper towel was there for him on the rug by my desk and he needed to get down from my lap to drink. He crouched in front of the bowl, when normally he would stand, and drank and drank

149

the cool water. He then lay down on the floor facing the bowl and periodically lapped water. We were there several hours. He alternated being held and lapping water. He did not attempt to jump onto the bed and cuddle down in his soft wildlife comforter. I prayed and prayed for him in many ways, including the Rosary. Though so sick, he still patted the beads as he lay on my lap. My tears fell all over his soft fur.

During this period alone I eventually asked if he would speak to me aside from the love and words we had been exchanging. I had paper and pen and as he lay in front of the water dish looking up at me periodically, I wrote furiously and quickly the message he was conveying to me. We had done this so many times these past years. Never before were his words more important than now. I filled two sides of a page from my legal pad and stopped as he stopped. Though I write the words I cannot fully comprehend the messages I receive from him until they end and I read them over slowly. I could barely read. I was just convulsing in tears over the horrible truth of his leaving me and the beauty of his message.

The words were all love and I feel I cannot share the entire message for it is so precious and personal, but I can share a segment of it. We had declared our love for each other over and over, and then he said,

> *You are my life. You have cared for me and loved me as no one else ever could. I shall be with you every moment. When you think you are alone you will not be. I will always be there. Hold my paws. I will reach out and give you my paw as I always have and you will know and feel its touch. We will never be separated. You are the love of my life and we are one heart and one soul. In Heaven we shall be together. I await you. Never feel alone.*

And too, He said—

> *Look at my quilt. See the indentation. Feel me on your legs at night holding your hands, sleeping, loving you. We have secrets no one knows. You are always with me in my heart. Hold my ashes. Feel my presence.*

He then added two things that were so overwhelming. In the rereading I could barely live let alone read. He said—

Thank you for holding me tomorrow, for being there. I will enter you in a way you could never dream and this bond is eternal.

I did not understand this but knew and believed I would learn the true meaning. Among other precious personal words to me he said:

I do not want to go. I am as surprised as you are. I do not want to go. But read this often—remember all our days and our last hours, and hold me in your heart and in your arms always.

I gathered him in my arms and just wept and wept. We then went downstairs for the evening where after I made Bob a light dinner, Chester lay on my legs all evening as we three spent our last night together of almost sixteen years. I ate no dinner because I was still fasting for Chester, as I had been all week. This would continue through Friday and the weekend, when I broke the fast on Sunday.

We eventually went to bed but I stayed awake all night as Chester laid on my legs as always. I sat up against the pillow so as to see him better with only a night light on. He held my hands with his paws as always and we communed and I cried and cried, and stroked his little head. I had given him his blessing on his forehead, the sign of the cross, as I had done every night of his life with me. He left me several times to lap water from his dish and then returned to my legs. When dawn came I did not want to disturb him. I wanted to spend our last day together as he wished it to be, and I would follow.

I had not far to follow for he seemed much weaker in the light of morning. He had not eaten all week. But we also knew because of the tumor he had very little time. I still prayed continuously for a miracle. He could barely get down and up onto the bed again now after drinking water. Bob felt he could best help by sending our requests for prayer by e-mail, and after spending time with us off and on, he went over to his office. When Rochester needed to drink his water, I quickly dressed and then picked him up and we sat on the bed together again, he on my legs facing me holding my hands. It was so precious. I look back on it again and again and am overwhelmed here in tears relating it. He never once stopped expressing his love to me.

This continued all day. We two stayed on the bed communing and holding hands. I prayed with him many times, talked lovingly in whispers, and little replies of love in the quiet would come, and I would lift him down periodically to lap water. He never used his litter box after Wednesday evening, further evidence that his dear little body was failing him and closing down. Though I prayed with *"laying on of hands"* many times still expecting a miracle, I did not receive the miracle I was praying for, that my little one would survive. Soon I began to pray that God would take him while we two were here together. Bob came to visit us periodically and to talk to him, pet him, and comfort me. I could not bear to look at the clock for time was ticking away and would take my beloved with it.

Finally at 4 PM I could stay no longer with him on the bed. I carried him into the living room and Bob and I each took our last pictures of him with us. I then asked Bob to trim some of his handsome marmalade fur from places it would not show so that I might always have it, and he did. Rochester laid in my arms as he cut it. I had already died within myself. I then gently kissed him and placed him in his carrier on a covering within and we went to the car. On the drive there the door to the carrier was open as before and I put my hand in so he could hold it and rest his head on his paws. We had traveled thousands of miles like that in the past years from Pennsylvania to New Hampshire and back. Never did I ever dream I would be making a final ride holding hands with my little beloved. There are no words to describe my agony on that trip as my eyes never left his dear little face, and my other hand stroked his forehead. And as the miles passed and time grew shorter I was praying he would pass away there in his little familiar carrier as we held hands. I was begging that he would die naturally without having to enter that clinic. Again my prayers were not answered.

It Takes Time

One can die of a broken heart.
　　You slip and slide downward
　　　　into the mire—
　　　　　　a quicksand pulling
　　　　　　　　you deeper and deeper
　　　　　　　　　　into sadness and despair.
There is nothing to cling to—
　　yet you reach out to grasp
　　　　again and again.
Your heart splits in two
　　and you submerge into the depths—
　　　　arms and hands upright
　　　　　　trying to cling to Heaven
　　　　　　　　to help you.
But you sink and sink
　　your own tears adding to
　　　　all that surrounds you—
　　　　　　all that pulls you down—
　　　　　　　　and then you are gone
　　　　　　　　　　into the unfathomable
　　　　　　　　　　　abyss.
　　　　One day you shall rise again—
　　　　　　but it takes time.

JGK

Rochester's Eternal Gift

It seems I have no tears left. They should have fallen—
Their ghosts, if tears have ghosts, did fall — that day.
—Edward Thomas, "Tears"

Friday evening, May 31, 2002

WE WALKED INTO THAT VETERINARIAN'S CLINIC at 5 PM on Friday, March 8th, and were directed to one of the small rooms. The three of us entered and a woman Veterinarian was there with a young assistant. There was no conversation except the doctor's instructions to wrap Rochester in a towel provided. I felt like I was in a nightmare and cannot imagine why I did not scream. I had thought yesterday while with him of we three just running away, that he would get well and what we were living through was not true. We took him from his carrier and like a robot I did what she asked not believing I was doing it. I laid him on the table and wrapped him in a tan towel like a baby. There was no time allowed. They wanted it done at once. In that moment I died a thousand deaths. I kissed him and whispered soft things to him and stood there holding him, the back of his little head against my cheek and his little paws lying over the towel. I can barely write this to tell you it is so devastating to me. I cannot see to write.

As his little head rested on me she quickly put a needle into his right paw and he was gone instantly. I do not know how I survived it. I wanted to go too. They wanted to take him from me and I said "*no,*" that I wanted to sit and hold him awhile. Bob stood by me and I sat down cradling him in my left arm like a baby. I could barely see him for my tears but his eyes were still open and he felt so tiny in the towel. I kept kissing his little face and soaking it in tears, and holding his little paws that I had held every day and night for so many years. I was out of my mind. His little stomach moved and made a little sound. These were gasses, but I thought he was still alive. Bob assured me it was not so.

Suddenly in the midst of all this pain and grief a word popped into my head, a word at that moment that I did not know the meaning of any more than I knew my own name at that moment. The word was "*Anima.*" Upon hearing the word mentally I instantly knew what I had to do. Bob just watched me saying nothing. *Barely able to see I began to give Rochester little kisses on his mouth, and then I gently opened his tiny mouth until it was substantially opened. I then placed my lips and mouth over his open mouth totally encasing it, and began to draw in deep breaths from Rochester. I knew I would carry his breath within me always. Over and over again I drew his breath into my body and kept doing this until I knew I was to stop. I knew I was doing a deeply spiritual act yet had only been led to do it moments before.*

I then kissed him and gently closed his dear little mouth and kissed his eyes and closed those too. He lay in my arms like the precious Angel he is and I just could not stop looking at him. By now my lips were tingling and felt unusual but nothing mattered but Rochester. I sat in the chair holding him while Bob asked the assistant twice when she returned to please allow us more time. I cannot write about that time with him in my arms, my final minutes of ever holding him in reality again. My heart was so broken I wanted to die. If I could have taken the needle for him I would have done that, or given him my liver. The moment came at 5:45 PM when I was forced to lay him in the arms of the assistant. As she stood in the hall with him I again wanted to snatch him and run. To part with his tiny body ripped my heart apart. I could not bear that it was my very last time to see him until we are together in Heaven. I died within seeing her turn and carry my little one away! Through my grief I asked her where she was taking him and when she replied I just turned and walked away. I was crazy inside! I wanted to die and be with him.

May no one else ever have to go through such pain. We had made arrangements for cremation but I cannot tell you when I did that. I only knew it had to be so, so that I might forever have his ashes, and then one day my ashes will be added and mixed with his, and hopefully Bob's too. We left the office and I cannot remember the drive home. It was an *"hour of lead,"* of experiencing a death of myself.

Once in the cottage in total grief I listened to what I was feeling within—inspired thoughts I know with a certainty. I believe Chester inspired me to draw his breath from him again and again. It had only entered my mind following the word *"Anima"* that had made its entrance also. I believe he inspired me to draw out his breath so that I might be a vessel and carrier of his breath to join us in the deepest way possible. Perhaps it was both God and Chester, and Mary too— and all the Angels. I am only so deeply grateful I obeyed without hesitation, acting on a word whose meaning I did not know then, and on instructions that appeared and I knew only that I was to follow, and wanted to follow with all my being.

When I looked up the word *"Anima"* in the dictionary the next day I was overwhelmed to learn it meant *"breath, soul."*

Forever I am carrying his breath and soul within me until we are together again. I look at the words I have written down in my tablet when we were together in our room Thursday, March 7th. He said to me:

> *Thank you for holding me tomorrow, for being there. I will enter you in a way you could never dream and this bond is eternal.*

He had told me what would happen but I could not understand then. I had only to obey what was being said to me within, as I stood holding his precious being in that Veterinarian's office. *He trusted me to know and obey, that is how close and one we were and are! He passed on to me the greatest treasure he could ever give to me, his very breath and soul to carry for him forever.* It is a gift that is so utterly divine and surprising and so cherished by me that it cannot be expressed in earthly words. I only know if I were offered all the wealth in the world it would seem ridiculous in light of the wealth I carry within. I have thought, *"what if I did not obey or understand?"* when that word and impulses to act were given? And then I conclude that that was not an option. After all our years together and our communication by thought and word, Rochester knew without a doubt I would *know and act*, even predicting it to me in his words on Thursday that I wrote down. We are so one he would not let me fail in my grief. He made it so emphatically known I acted immediately. I offer daily much thanksgiving for Rochester's eternal gift to me.

To have this happen is sacred and other worldly, but that is how I live. Life has been that way since March 8th. Life has always been that way in the presence of Rochester.

Still yet another blessing of such worth was awaiting upon our arrival home that night of March 8th, that night that seems unreal. Bob went over to his office to send several e-mails to family and to the staff at Blue Dolphin Publishing. As he went online to send the e-mail of Rochester's passing to my publisher and staff there was one awaiting him there from Blue Dolphin, from my friend Chris Comins. Chris's message stated that at 5:10 PM he had a *vision of Rochester in the center of a circle of Angels and Light.* He wanted to know if Rochester was all right. Rochester had passed at 5:07 PM in my arms and Chris saw him in this heavenly state at 5:10 PM, not knowing of all that was transpiring here in New Hampshire 3,000 miles from him in California. I cannot express what this vision has continued to mean to me and the peace it gives to me. I know Rochester is safely in Heaven awaiting the day we will be reunited.

This vision has sustained me since March 8th, for every night since September 1989 Chester has fallen asleep *"in a ring"* of etherial music titled *"The Fairy Ring."* I have written of it in an earlier entry. Fairies are deva, lower than the angels yet a form of angels, of the spiritual world. I believe the Angels cared for my little angel in the most tender of ways making his passage filled with love and memories of the countless precious nights we two spent *"in The Fairy Ring,"* together. And soon, very soon, we shall spend every night there together again, for I still have been hesitant to listen. The cassette still sits in the tape player waiting for the night when Chester and I will forever share our music once more.

Chris has continued to help and support me in the weeks that followed via e-mail, and too, has had numerous messages for me specifically about Rochester. I am so grateful for all he has done and continues to do. Not only does he very wonderfully see that Rochester's and my books get out into the world, but he gave confirmation that my beloved little Rochester entered into another world of eternal life and love and glory. That confirmation is a divine gift, confirming all I believed to be true for Rochester before receiving the confirmation.

These two supernatural happenings of March 8th, my carrying now Rochester's "*Anima*," and his encounter with "*Angels and Light*" that carried him to Heaven, have been my sustaining strength in the past days and weeks since March 8th, and will be in what life I have here on earth ahead. We shall be together again forever in Heaven, and while I await I carry him within and live with his spirit.

In a previous book of mine I wrote these words about Rochester.

He is enchantment, and his presence lights up my existence! Angels do that! We share our moments and days and because of him I am a finer and better person. He is an Angel, my shining Star sent by God.

I have always believed he is an Angel. That belief can never be shaken. He has always too—been a shining Star in my life, for he has lightened my heart and soul all these past years and travelled a healing path with me. He has brightened my existence with the light and height and depth of his love. He continues to do so and always shall.

Soon after we arrived home the evening of March 8th, and after learning of the vision, in my brokenness I looked up at the night sky and knew my little one was taken in a circle of *Light and Angels to God*— *Rochester is my shining star, my Angel.*

It seems so right to include this poem I wrote for his May 30th birthday in 1998.

MY STAR

I gaze up at the heavens
    and see the brilliant, shimmering stars
        in the night sky—
And in wonder feel that I
    am one
        with all creation.
And yet this inward elation
    cannot compare
        to what I feel

When I gaze upon the radiant star
who shares my nights and days -
shining his love in tender ways
everywhere we are!
He is my Angel of Light
my one true star—
more beauteous
than all the stars of night.

For Rochester   JGK
with inexpressible love on his birthday
May 30, 1998—and for all time—

And this night of May 31st at 5 PM I again keep my hour vigil with
him, in tears, and turning again to the Rosary and the comfort of those
repetitive prayers, I know Mary is with us. I look from time to time at
Rochester's comforter across from me on the bed. His floral tin of ashes
sits on the spread next to it. He is with me as strongly as if I could see his
blessed little body of marmalade fur on the quilt, and his golden eyes
gazing at me in love. It shall always be so.

Rochester still naps in the middle of his wildlife quilt in our wiriting room.
The indentation of his sweet body is still there.

My Father's Birthday

HEARTBEAT

For ten years after he died—with pride—
I wore my father's large watch.
And though I often cried—the watch somehow denied
His death to me. His absence was like a dark blotch
Upon my life—and to see his watch there
Upon my wrist, to hear its soft sound,
Was like unspoken prayer—
And comfort to me each time it was wound.
A part of him went everywhere with me
And helped to regulate my existence.
A mere touch or glance upon the face and I knew it was he
Giving his time—his love—from an unknown distance.

Then one day his watch died too!
And I knew—it was true.
I would have to go on without this blessed reminder
That had not ceased whispering since he lived—this physical binder
Of his life to mine—
A very tangible sign—
Of this man most cherished.
His ticking watch had nourished
My soul.
Symbolic of his beating heart—it played its role.
At least I still have this lifeless gold
To hold.

Dedicated to my Dad
Ellis George Gray
Died August 21, 1977

JGK
August 16, 1993
New Hampshire

160

Sunday, June 2, 2002

HOUGH THIS BOOK, this journal, is written for and about my Rochester, it seems right to include the poem that opens this meditation.
Today is my Dad's birthday and though he died in 1977 his presence is
ever alive to me each day. I still write poems for him, journal entries
about him, speak of him in my books, and ask his intercession in prayer.
He appears too in my dreams. He is very real and present. It is my Dad as
well as Mary, our Blessed Mother, that I have asked to take care of my
beloved Rochester until I join them in Heaven. Therefore my Dad
belongs in Rochester's book. He loved and cared about our family cat ,
Mitzi, so deeply when I was growing up, as did I, that twenty-one years
after Mitzi's death, and following my Dad's and Mother's deaths thirteen
months apart, I learned a precious secret. My Dad's wallet and little
notebook he always carried became mine. Inside the notebook encircled
by a fat rubber band, on a small and neatly folded piece of paper, I
discovered how deep was his love for Mitzi. Even the rubber band stood
the test of time. I hold this paper of his in my hand now. In two months
it will be forty-six years old. Written in his neat small hand writing are
these words.

Wednesday—
August 22nd—1956
at 8:30 PM
Mitzi

He carried this paper for twenty-one years until his own death when
he joined Mitzi in Heaven! These words of his had recorded Mitzi's
departure. He died August 21st, one day before she did, but over two
decades later. I know he was grief stricken, and I too shared in his grief.

It is a long a story to relate here but I honor my Dad even more for his
love of our Mitzi and his continued sorrow over her death. Mitzi, a black
Persian, appears in my books *Enchantment of Writing* and *Compassion for
All Creatures* through word and a small picture. The same picture in color
and framed is in our living room this day and has been for many years.

Along with the small memorial to Mitzi on paper, my Dad also
carried a drawing I had made for him. As the years pass I realize how very
much I am like him emotionally, and in cherishing beings and memories
and tangible keepsakes of theirs. That he needed to put into writing his

deep sorrow, though only a few words, tells in a brief cameo what I am trying to express in writing this book.

The words of Isak Dinesen have touched me for some years. She writes:

> *All sorrows can be borne if you put them into a story or tell a story about them.*

I am attempting to tell Rochester's and my story, and my Dad told his in condensed form. His few words spoke volumes.

It is no mystery then that my Dad's large watch was a treasure to me. I wore it after his and my Mother's deaths for ten years though it was a man's watch. It meant so very much to me. The poem expresses this far better than I can at this moment. When it could not be repaired, for I tried to have this done, I still wore it long after. Several years. Then I put it safely away.

I write about this now because it is similar to my wearing Rochester's red collar that is ever on my arm since he physically left. There has been no day or night that I have not worn this collar. It is worn even in bed, for it was always there on Rochester's sweet neck as he slept on my legs. It is part of me and always shall be. It does not tick like my Dad's watch but has a heart beat of its own that only I know and recognize, for I held its owner in my arms each day and night for almost sixteen years.

Recently I read about a man who lost his wife on September 11th when the twin towers fell to earth. He ran into the streets from his office building to find her, even though she was within the first tower. He knew she was gone yet could not give up hope. As he sat on a curb covered in ashes he saw a woman's chain bracelet in the debris in the street. He slipped it on his arm and wears it continuously, never removing it. It is a link to that horrendous day and to his dear wife he never found. Grief and sorrow change us. The need for some physical connection to our loved one and the events of their passing is essential.

And so on this day of my Dad's birthday we hang a new Hummingbird feeder in his honor just as we did just a couple of years ago. I had bought one back then after being inspired by the movie *Fearless* on television in which two persons who star in it buy gifts for their dead in order to aid in their own healing. Having survived a plane crash they are trying to help each other survive life in the aftermath of trauma they are experiencing. The things I have done and written about throughout this book were to help me survive also, and to honor Rochester. Now today too, to honor my Dad as well.

My Dad enjoyed watching the birds just as Rochester did, and also caring for a small garden. Rochester enjoys viewing his garden here. Several years ago I also gave two books to my Dad with the Hummingbird Feeder, for he loved to read. I placed them in my writing room in his honor for it is also a guest room and guests could enjoy them. I had a ceremony back then and lit candles, and displayed the gifts on our long wooden kitchen table along with Rochester's birthday gifts, for we were still celebrating his birthday on June 2nd. I never celebrated it only on May 30th. I prayed over the gifts to bless them and I took pictures of the display with Rochester amongst the gifts (he is my gift!) and especially with the books. He is fond of books and is an author himself. And my Dad would have loved Chester in life. He knows and cares for him now in Heaven.

As before when we hung the feeder, within a very short time a Hummingbird came to enjoy it. Back then I felt it was the spirit of my Dad coming to that first feeder, and today I feel it is he also. Minutes later another one arrives and I claim it as Rochester's spirit, temporarily in that form, to comfort and delight us.

Presenting another gift to my Dad is heartwarming and the gift brings his presence closer. I feel like a child again who surprises him, or the teenager, or the grown daughter. One of our daughters, Laurel, shares his birth date just as our daughter Janna shares hers of May 30th with Rochester. It is a family day that is both tearful and comforting. If only Rochester's precious earthly body was at the window viewing the Hummingbird feeder as before. But he *is* there.

Woodland Paths

My position is that you cannot and should not sever the ties.
Your loved one is in your heart, in your soul, and wrapped intrinsically
into who and what you are. You will spend the rest of your life
remembering, internalizing, and renegotiating all that
this loss means to you in this lifetime.
—Ashley Davis Prend, A.C.S.W.

Wednesday, June 5, 2002

WHEN YOU ARE GRIEVING try to go off alone into nature regularly. Take a walk by the sea or by a lake. Very especially take a walk in the woods by yourself. If there is not one close by, take a drive and try to find one. It will be a refuge. Your grief will not leave but you will feel like a different person there surrounded by the trees and woodland paths, the singing birds, the small creatures, and too, the healing color green. You will be a different person than you are when in the company of others. You need to be your true self.

We live in and are surrounded by woods with the glistening lake in front of our cottage, and it is here in these woods we love that I am with Rochester always. I need to be here! When I lived in Pennsylvania I always needed to be here. When you go into the woods talk to your loved one aloud, be the beloved individual human or animal. Expect your loved one to hear and feel the freedom to use your voice. I do this in the wooded areas, in my prayer chair by the lake, but indoors as well. I talk aloud to

Chester many times a day just as I did when he was visibly here. I acknowledge his spiritual presence daily by using my audible voice. It helps me to do this and I feel it is paying him honor and acknowledging that I believe with all my heart that he is very present to me in spirit. I talk to him continually mind to mind, heart to heart also as I have always done, but I feel it is worthy and healthy to talk aloud to my beloved little one. It is comforting to read in several other sources also that this is not an unusual thing to do and brings a certain indefinable peace.

As a little girl I talked aloud to my dolls and my stuffed animals. I sensed a spirit within them and treated them with respect. Now I know with undebatable certainty that Rochester's spiritual presence is continually with me, and I talk to him not needing his visible body to authenticate what we are experiencing together. It is not a land of pretend. He is here. He is real.

An alcoholic is never fully recovered even though he may have stopped drinking years before and may never drink again. I have read that to grieve is like being in this same state, for I will forever be grieving and affected by Rochester's physical absence. I do not believe there is an end to grieving and mourning. We are living a new kind of life, a new kind of relationship. Even if it were possible I could not comprehend putting an end to my grief for Rochester. Not ever. He lives! He is simply invisible, although not always! He has made certain I have seen him many times. He communicates. He is here in great love as always.

I believe as do others, that you will forever have a relationship with your loved one that has gone before you to Heaven if you so choose. Many block out any hope of that for various reasons, and too, perhaps the relationship was difficult or hurtful when it existed on earth. And many want to have a quick fix or a stated process in recovering from grief. Some even seem to wipe out grief rather quickly and pretend things are as they were. I know such people, be the grief for humans or animals. Actually I know several where there was simply no evidence of grief at the time, or long after, or for as long as I have known them. But I believe that grief changes your life and continues to change it. I will always be influenced for good and in every way by the love I shared and continue to share with Rochester. I bear a holy mark and imprinting of grief as do many who loved so deeply, and this is continuous. And it *will continue* to change my life. I see that every day.

Grief is not something we as human beings get over,
Instead it is something we live with.
                    —Dr. Allan D. Wolfelt, *Understanding Grief*

Rochester enjoying his view of lake and woods

Maya

No wise man who ever lived could truly comfort the heart
that has lost what it held most dear.
Love—in any form—can never be replaced.

—Martin Scot Kosins

Sunday, June 9, 2002

JUST A COUPLE OF YEARS AGO I discovered a book of extraordinary love. It is a book I treasure because I respect the author so deeply, and that he bared his soul. It is a uniquely precious book of inspiration for anyone who has ever loved and lost an animal companion. I first mentioned it in my *Journal of Love* and now once again must write about it. It is titled *Maya's First Rose: Diary of a Very Special Love* by Martin Scot Kosins. The author loved his dog for eighteen wondrous years before she died of old age, but she outlived her life expectancy because of the incredible love of her wonderful companion. Martin's most important goal was to keep Maya joyful and alive in her final years. He sacrificed career and friends only wishing to be with Maya. Others did not understand, but he did not care for he loved his beloved Maya so dearly. Martin and Maya would sit shoulder to shoulder. They gazed together straight ahead watching all of nature and listening to the call of the geese. There, on an old Army blanket beneath a small tree that stood beneath ancient pines, Martin and Maya shared love that cannot be put into words. Martin writes, *"There was no us anymore. We had become one. Our hearts had a single beat. And our lives a single purpose—the care and companionship of each other."* I too can say all of these words about Rochester and myself, *"There was no us anymore. We had become one. Our hearts had a single beat."*

Their deep communication existed and shall live in their hearts forever. I have read this book through tears, many times before Rochester went to Heaven, and many times since then. I often carry it around with me in our cottage. It is the greatest of consolation, for Martin's thoughts capture my deepest thoughts about Rochester. I have given many copies as gifts and you will be blessed if you own it and read it.

Before Rochester left I would cry in the reading of it, devastated for Martin at Maya's leaving, but also because of the great tenderness and beauty of their love. Too, I could not comprehend how I could live through Rochester's leaving as Martin was forced to do in Maya's passing. He is the only one I knew then who loves his blessed animal companion as I love Rochester. Others did not, and still do not, understand my great love for Rochester. But I do not care, for though it often stings, I know God gave me a beloved animal companion and a great treasure to love and cherish, and Rochester too, loves me so.

At one point when Martin was forced to leave Maya at the Veterinarian he writes:

> *I realized for the first time that this was not a dog, a pet, I was leaving behind. It was a part of me. As dear as my heart was to my body, that is how dear Maya had become to my life.*

I too felt this silent terror in me and inexpressible love and oneness with him as I was forced to leave my Rochester there in the Veterinarian's office, and Martin's words are mine also. But I had felt it all long before this day and in our daily life we shared. Like Martin, I never wanted to leave Rochester, except for necessary errands. He writes that the world understands less the pain of losing an animal for many have not felt for themselves the true love of an animal. He states:

> *So you cannot really expect these people to realize that your love for a pet may be greater than your love for the dearest people in your life. The bond*

*is different, and can never be put into words. It is a bond that only The
Heart understands.*

This composer whose music has been performed and recorded
internationally writes in this his first book, after telling that his mother
had died some time before Maya, *"No one ever asked me, Are you getting
another Mother?"* Yet he regularly heard from people he knew asking,
"Are you getting another dog?"

Like myself he feels there is great lack of understanding in the world
when a precious animal companion passes on.

His writings are an enormous comfort and consolation that I read
portions from each day, spiritual medicine for the heart and soul written
by someone who knows the mysteries of creature-human bonding and
their eternal love.

Like myself with Rochester's, he keeps her belongings and toys in
view, and her leash still hanging on a door knob. He deeply shares much
more.

I know now why I was meant to discover this book at my wonderful
Bookland store in Maine, where Rochester's picture on the cover of my
own book was displayed so very close to Maya. On some other plane, in
some other realm there was a connection. And now Maya and her Martin
are my companions in grief. With Martin I write his words about Maya's
passing that he has unknowingly given to me—

if I did not exactly die that night, I know I was certainly not alive

Learning to Live

Tears may be dried up, but the heart never.

—Unknown

Tuesday, June 11, 2002

WHATEVER IT IS THAT SOOTHES AND SUSTAINS US should be incorporated into our lives in grief. Recently on *Nightline* we saw the story of a man grieving over the death of his son in the tragedy of 9/11. This man immersed himself in the music that he and his son, his only child, mutually loved. Again and again he would play it as I had played Rochester's and my tape of *"The Fairy Ring"* nightly since 1989. Now I cannot play it, but this man's soul needed to hear his special music at once, after his loss and in the months following. He listened to it at night alone after days of working to help rebuild the Pentagon where his son had worked and died. This was not his normal work for he had retired. He worked the days that he could, even turning to drinking at times in the pain, and lived in a trailer near by, having moved down there from a close by state. Alone in the nights he played his music and cried. His small desk was covered with a display of framed pictures of his son. He could barely talk in his grief when being interviewed. We all do what we have to do to gain solace and help ourselves. I cried with this man in his desolation.

We do not have to explain to others what we are doing or why. Some people need to sew or knit, others to go away to places once shared with their lost loved ones, others need to be by the sea, or in the mountains,

170

others by a lake. Others paint, stare into space, or watch the stars. It does not have to cost anything. We do not have to prove ourselves to others or that the things we are doing are nourishing or calming. The important thing is how it makes us feel. It is a gift to ourselves.

When my Dad suddenly died in August of 1977, my Mother was lost, and his death was followed in a very brief period by her brother's death. The three of them were extremely close. Though she was a business woman and was always active, she was deeply grieving. Often she did not want us to come near her. Her personality even was different at times. The one thing she did enjoy was to come to New Hampshire with us over Thanksgiving that year, and she deeply was moved by the glorious sunsets over our lake. All the while she was here she was knitting and crocheting. When she died thirteen months after my Dad from a broken heart, we found a treasure. In their den behind their two recliners were literally piles of beautiful handmade shawls of every color imaginable! Some had notes pinned on them to tell me who they had been created for, but most were just neatly piled there. With great love I gradually dispensed them to our daughters, my Mother's many friends, and years later to several young granddaughters that had been born. Though they could not use them then, they would have them as a keepsake when older. I had never before seen so many handmade items stacked together in one place, and all created in less than a year by the hands of a woman so deeply in grief, mourning the loss of her husband. She had left a legacy from her heart to family and friends, and even to strangers. It still goes on. And all the shawls were created in the evenings, for during the days she still worked part time and also had the sad job of cleaning out her brother's home with our occasional help. Even in that she wanted to do as much of it alone as possible, and we honored her in this only doing what she wished us to do. It was all part of her grieving process. I see that more clearly now.

Writing this book for Rochester and myself is a gift to us, but it is also meant to be a gift to all those who grieve who read this book or who will one day deeply grieve. It is our legacy of love. It comes from the heart and soul. It comes from the depths of grief with love. Everyone needs solace. Too, in the months of writing this Journal I have attempted to help others who have lost animals and humans by writing letters, cards, and by sending Journals. I did not impose myself, but let them know I was there in prayer. There is a fine line we have to recognize, even though we may want to do more. To impose ourselves physically or by phone is often intrusive on grief. Other people do need people around, others need them at a distance, just knowing there *is* someone if they do need them.

In a small community in New Jersey near where the twin towers fell, there are many widows because of this tragedy. Many with new babies and young children. They are struggling to go on, even months later, after losing husbands and the fathers to their children, and their brothers. They meet once a week in each others' homes to light many candles, display their loved ones' framed pictures near the candles, share stories, and cry and cry. They are deeply in grief. They share good also and just need to "be" in each other's company. They are learning to live while grieving.

Too, a Mother in another state has kept her son's room exactly as it was when he died September 11th. She often goes in to sit on his bed or in a chair to read or pray. On this news program his picture is seen above the bed, and his sweet dog is shown lying under the bed just near the edge, his little face on his paws looking out from dear sad eyes. This little dog is waiting for his master to come back. We are told it is where he has been waiting since September 11th. Animals too grieve so deeply, just as humans. This little dog has been mourning for months and months, his little heart shattered in grief.

And because someone with little or no experience of having lost an irreplaceable loved one tells us we must be brave, does not mean we have to be brave. Courage and bravery do not come before grieving. Love is more important and our grief. Courage surely is needed as we grieve and enter this strange land, *"this land of tears,"* and reside there indefinitely , but it should not take the place of grief. Listen to your own heart and advice and grieve for your loved one in the way that fits your nature. For if you do not, you cannot go on. Do not listen to others who do not understand, and are uncomfortable because you grieve. You will carry a lump of despair within until you travel your own personal passage and learn to live with this grief.

Rituals may seem mad from the outsider's point of view.

—Unknown

Rings of Solace

The soul never thinks without an image.

—Aristotle

What a moment that was! Everything was bright with light,
and there was a sound like the rustling of a million angel's wings,
and there was singing everywhere.

—Dale Evans Rogers, *Angel Unaware*

Friday, June 14, 2002

*W*HEN I WENT BACK THROUGH STENO PADS that I had made continuous notes in concerning all things that happened March 7th and 8th and earlier that week, I discovered a startling page. I had not seen it in all these weeks while writing in my journal and writing this journal book because I could not bear to look at the notes I made in that period. Once entering it all in my journal briefly to expand on later, I did not go back to those pages there or in my steno pad. The memories of it all are so painful I had to place what occurred those days at the end of this book. I was not strong enough to read my notes. I still was not strong enough to write it all and then to proof read it. I just sat sobbing and sobbing all through the writing and reading of those last entries. I still do. I always will.

One of the pages I discovered with my notes was a drawing. Often I draw things I am praying about. On the page was a circle and in the

middle lengthwise I had written Rochester's name. On the circle around
his name I had written ten other names, each horizontally across the line
of the circle with a name too at top and bottom. I had begun with my
Dad's name at the left side and went counter clockwise around when I
devised it. I do not know why I did it that way. I was broken, and I had
created it up in my writing room with Rochester after we had brought him
home from the Veterinarian's clinic that Thursday afternoon of March
7th. As he lay on my lap at one point I drew that diagram. I entered on
it names of ten men I had sincerely and devotedly prayed for and with,
over a period of fifteen years in the late 1970s, the 1980s, and into the
1990s. With the exception of two they were all my Dad's age or a bit
older. The other two were close friends of mine I have written about in
my books; one six years older than myself and the other fifteen years
younger. All had eventually died of serious problems, and one took his
own life, but all deeply appreciated my prayers often, and always I prayed
for them when apart from them. Many had recovered and remained well
for years.

That afternoon of March 7th in my writing room I *"laid hands"* on the
circle and prayed and asked Jesus to heal Rochester as I *"laid hands"* on
him also, and I asked these men in Heaven for their intercession for
Rochester, beginning with my Dad and Uncle. No, I did not ask, I *begged!*
Somehow I expected a miracle.

That circle of prayer warriors for Rochester became important to me
as the hours passed as I frequently turned to these intercessors again and
again. I just believed they would help me and I believe that they did
intercede. But the answer I was pleading for was not to be.

Now weeks later I find this diagram of a ring or circle of prayer
warriors with Rochester in the center and I am struck by a realization!

At 5:10 PM on Friday, March 8th, my friend Chris Comins in
California had a vision of Rochester within a circle or ring of *Angels and
Light* not knowing anything about the serious situation with Rochester.
What an incredible synchronism. I placed Rochester in a ring, by faith,
through drawing and prayer on Thursday, about twenty-four hours
before Chris had the vision of Rochester in the ring of *Angels of Light* at
5:10 PM Friday. Such mysteries! Not explainable—yet I cannot help but
believe that there is some mystical connection. Perhaps one circle was to
prepare Rochester for his leaving, and the other circle was to transport

him to Heaven. This is my belief—most definitely, of the circle of *Angels and Light* Chris saw around Rochester. These Angels truly transported him to Heaven! The other I can only ponder and wonder about, yet somehow feel there is a mysterious and Heavenly connection. One day I shall know about it all when I am reunited in Heaven with Chester. That ring of *Angels and Light* surrounding my Rochester is an enormous solace, and a comfort so great it is not expressible. I turn to it in thought, tears, and prayer many times a day since Rochester left, and have often reread Chris's e-mail telling me of it on that terrible Friday night of March 8th. Later I would write a poem in gratitude for the solace of this vision, and for Chris and his gift to me—and continued support these past months. But the vision was from God—God who is within us all, humans and animals, our very essence. I saw Him in Rochester's golden eyes and felt His presence in Rochester. God is everywhere and too most surely in Heaven. There is no adequate expression of gratitude, surely not a poem, although it is one form of my prayers of attempted and deep gratitude.

THE VISION

My friend had a vision
That Rochester had risen
In a ring of Angels and Light—
He was lifted in love
To God above
On a tear-filled and dark Friday night.

My friend did not know
Of my sadness and woe
Or that Rochester was fading and ill
He saw only release
And Rochester at peace
Apparently fulfilling God's will.

The vision of glory
That adds to his story
That is day by day ever on-going—

Gives peace to my heart
While we're briefly apart
And his presence on me he's bestowing.

For beloved Rochester   JGK
and in deep gratitude   June 2002
to Chris Comins

The Rosary too is a circle of precious love that encircles Rochester several times daily as I pray for him, and one that had encircled him spiritually since he was a kitten. I believe Mary encircles Rochester in her arms many times as he awaits with my Dad for me to one day be there too.

Each reader who grieves over an animal companion or person will somehow be given a blessing of comfort too. Often it is not evident at first, especially when one is in pain and grief, but through prayer ask that you be shown a loving moment or symbol that you may have been given and overlooked that you can hold on to in your grieving and forever in regard to your loved one. When you learn what it is write it on your heart in gratitude and into your journal for all time. One day soon when I am finished writing this book I will make a drawing or painting of my interpretation of Chris's vision of Rochester in the ring of *Angels and Light*. I see it often in prayer, the image I have been given of it.

It will be an icon of love for me, a visual attempt of a deeply mystical occurrence that took place, that I carry in my mind and heart forever until Chester and I are together once more.

Too, another ring of love and solace to me is Rochester's red collar that encircles my left arm forever, buckled into the same little hole that it was when around his neck, and never, ever unbuckled. His purple collar also remains buckled into the same hole, an eternal circle that lies on his quilt by day and my nighttable by night.

Years ago Chester and I were also given the ethereal music of "The Fairy Ring" that we entered together before sleep each night, music I have written about in a previous meditation. This composition was so hauntingly overwhelming we never tired of it for twelve and a half years! A circle or ring is symbolic of endless love, the love that Rochester and I experience and have been given by God, and that is watched over and protected by Mary and the Angels.

NIGHT TRAVEL

My beloved little Rochester
longs to gently float in spirit—
When it's time to board the strain
he cuddles then to hear it.
And as we listen together
we are each a stowaway—
The music washes over us
in haunting communique.

Dedicated with love to Rochester   JGK
Written as we listened to
The Fairy Ring

The Fairy Ring is our music, our song. It is a blessing to us. And Rochester is pure blessing to me above any music.

It is another Friday. I write this meditation of the *"rings"* on still yet another Friday, one that is no different in intensity of grief and loss than all the previous ones. I have spent an hour in prayer and tears in our writing room from five to six PM as I make this vigil with Rochester and his transport to Heaven. Often I pray the Rosary aloud during this Holy Hour each Friday as I hold his flowered tin containing his ashes. My own voice in prayer drowns out and suppresses the image in my mind of Rochester's last moments. I stare at his empty wildlife quilt or close my eyes envisioning his precious body lying there in peaceful sleep. Through the Rosary I feel an inexpressible oneness with Rochester in Heaven, though I daily live with his beloved spirit and Anima.

How comforting to me and unexplainable that years ago I was shown in prayer the names of our Guardian Angels. Rochester's Angel is Rosec. The letters are from his name and were given to me vividly in this unusual spelling across my inner forehead. I feel now in past weeks it spiritually ties in with my deep intensity and utter desire, and almost compulsion to daily pray the Rosary multiple times for him. The first three letters in each name are part of each other, just as he and I are part of each other. And *Mary* is my chosen confirmation name so many years ago. We belong to each other, we are one. And we belong to Mary.

We who choose to surround ourselves with lives even more temporary than our own, live within a fragile circle, easily and often breached. Unable to accept its awful gaps, we still would live no other way. We cherish memory as the only certain immortality never fully understanding the necessary plan.

—Irving Townsend, *The Once Again Prince*

Polar Bear

I do believe that we and our animals will meet again. If we do not,
and where we go is supposed to be heaven, it will not be heaven to me,
and it will not be where I wish to go.
—Cleveland Amory, The Best Cat Ever

Wednesday, June 19, 2002

THE ABOVE WORDS are truly ones that I agree with and say "amen" to with all my heart. They are written by a humanitarian and animal defender and I feel I must include him in Rochester's journal. His four books I own are right above my head on a bookshelf along the side of our bed and Rochester saw them every night before sleep. These double tiered book shelves wrap around two walls of our room and are filled with several hundred books all bought and read and referred to often in my life time with Chester. I cannot answer why I did not take these four special books down from the shelf in the weeks following Rochester's passing for I read each multiple times and enjoyed them so, and deeply admired this man's work with animals. I even referred to them in this book in my Journal Entry of Sunday, April 7th. In my sadness I just did not see them though they were right in front of me. This shows how grief can change you so and almost keep you oblivious of things around you, even things that would benefit you. How I would have loved to have read them in these preceding weeks.

Like Martin and Maya, who came into my life only a few years ago, Cleveland Amory and his beloved white cat Polar Bear also have an

179

eternal love affair, but they entered my life in 1986 very shortly after Rochester. I was given Cleveland's first book, *The Cat Who Came for Christmas,* by my friend Ruth as soon as she learned about Rochester. Eventually others gave me copies too which I shared. Before I could buy his second in the trilogy, *The Cat and the Curmudgeon,* Ruth also presented me with that. It was wonderful. I bought his third about Polar Bear, *The Best Cat Ever,* soon after it came into stores in 1993. This book includes the passing of Polar Bear and Cleveland's enormous grief. Polar Bear too lived the same amount of years on earth as Rochester—and like Martin for Maya and I for Rochester, Cleveland loved his dear Polar Bear with this same depth and undying intensity.

Polar Bear's final resting place is *"Fund for Animals" Black Beauty Ranch,* which over the years has become home to thousands of abused or abandoned animals. Cleveland began this *"Fund for Animals"* in 1967. Polar Bear has a fine headstone there at the Ranch with a most loving inscription about him. The last line reads: *"Til We Meet Again"*

Cleveland writes that he chose that line from the hymn "May the Good Lord Bless and Keep You." In discussing that line on the headstone in his book it was then he made the statement in the quotation that opens this entry. Another writer has also declared her beliefs in this regard. Anna Hemstead Branch stated in her small but powerful poem, "To a Dog":

> *If there is no God for thee—*
> *Then there is no God for me.*

I will not discuss heaven and animals here because I have written about it all earlier in this book, and in another of my books, and I am firm about my beliefs as is Cleveland. He writes about an argument with a Catholic Priest over this matter and Cleveland would not be moved. Nor will I. His very words in closing his book reaffirm his belief in the words on the monument of meeting Polar Bear again in Heaven. He ends his Introduction in the book with these moving words, *"Where he is really buried, and where he is, and where he will always be, is my heart."*

I am not alone in grieving deeply for Rochester, a precious animal companion, for I have read of the deep and on-going grief of Martin for Maya, and Cleveland for Polar Bear. Cleveland devoted his life to caring for other animals too, on his Ranch and in rescues. He writes about his Polar Bear, "*Certainly in just knowing Polar Bear, let alone being owned by him, I feel I owed him more than I could ever repay, let alone say.*" He goes on to write he was to him and will always be "*the best cat ever,*" though he knows many feel that about their cat. He always called Polar Bear that loving name in their special moments together. I too have loving names and phrases for Rochester.

I have written about Cleveland Amory in my book *Journal of Love* also and tell that in the Fall of 1998 Cleveland too passed away. This truly affected me. He was such a good and humane person and loved his precious Polar Bear with such a depth of love. I share in my book that he has been called "*the premier protector of animals on this planet.*" He has inspired motivated and blessed me by his trilogy of books and his actions for animal welfare. He has rescued countless animals who were mistreated or simply found to be "*inconvenient,*" and saved them from death's door to be given a new home at his unique sanctuary. It was his childhood ambition after reading the book "*Black Beauty*" to establish such a place, and he named it *Black Beauty Ranch*. It is in East Texas, and is a home where animals can live out their lives in dignity, knowing, as the last line of the book *Black Beauty* states, "*My troubles are all over, and I am at home.*" I too, had read and loved *Black Beauty* by Anna Sewell and was affected by it, but I had not read it until I was an adult. As a young girl I had also read *Beautiful Joe* and it left its mark on me. It is written by Marshall Saunders. As well as telling the life stories of a horse (Black Beauty) and dog (Beautiful Joe), these books reveal the terrible cruelties and injustices to animals, and are written messages to the world in the hope of stopping such atrocities and to learn kindness and compassion to all God's creatures.

Cleveland, too, loved the book *Beautiful Joe* that I have loved by the Canadian author, and he also mentions these two books as have I in *Journal of Love*. They are written about in his last book, *Ranch of Dreams—The Heartwarming Story of America's Most Unusual Animal Sanctuary*. I deeply recommend *Ranch of Dreams* and his *Polar Bear* trilogy. This man has left his mark for all time on behalf of animals and is sadly missed. His books are so worthy of reading and rereading which I continue to do, and this night I will begin anew *The Best Cat Ever*. I need to read the last book first so we may grieve together. I have to more fully share in his grief, for when I read it the first several times I had not lived it as he did and I had to force thoughts away that made me apply them to Rochester. In just glancing in the final pages I read through tears how he and a friend spoke not a word on Polar Bear's final trip to the veterinarian. Too, he not only wanted to be in the room with Polar Bear for his final injection but holding him also as he lay on a table. He writes: "*In what seemed just a few seconds it was all over*" and then he writes words that sear my mind and heart for similar ones affect me every day along with images of Rochester's last moments.

> *I only hope that someday I shall forget that part of my memory which tells me that I was part of doing something wrong to him, but rather there will remain only the memory that I was part of doing something that had to be done.*

He openly wept there in the office and could not stop weeping then or in long weeks ahead. Both Rochester and Polar Bear would have suffered had we allowed them to linger because we could not bear them to leave out of our enormous love for them. And though we did what had to be done because of that enormous love, it still is so painful to relive. It is so terrible. I fall apart just writing this.

Now Cleveland is with his beloved Polar Bear in Heaven. There is no question in my mind whatsoever about that. How grateful I am that this good man is living out eternally his belief and wish with his dearest companion, as Martin will with Maya , and I with Rochester. How thankful I am to both Cleveland Amory and Martin Scot Kosins my companions in grief, for baring their souls and allowing me to enter into their grieving.

A New Leg
of My Journey

Walkers who undertook pilgrimages to the Holy Land, la Sainte Terre,
came to be known as Sainte-Terrers. *Anyone who journeys*
toward spiritual and physical well-being
earns the name of Sainte-Terrer.
    —Carolyn Scott Kortge, *The Spirited Walker*

Thursday, June 20, 2002

I READ THAT OUR BODY HAS MEMORIES STORED IN EVERY CELL and that is why we know the term *"cellular memory."* Too, that traumatic events can shape the way we feel, act and think. To release and process these related memories is vital for our health.

I am slowly realizing that my cramped legs and back may have everything to do with my grieving. The death of a loved one can affect us deeply, and physical symptoms are often the result of emotional trauma. I know this from past experience. I have read that tears and emotional release lower blood pressure and heart rate, and if that be true then my health should be good in those areas. But my legs in particular are often not working properly and I have to force myself to "walk through it" up and down stairs and around the house. Again they tighten after I have been writing here in this Journal long hours. Since I have never had problems of this nature before in anyway and have been writing for years, and walking is something I enjoy, I am realizing that emotional pain has caused this tightness. It is as if a little light bulb suddenly appeared over my frazzled mind and head. And I believe Rochester pulled the little cord to light it! He has taught me numerous things about health in the past that I have included in my books.

I will say chants and affirmations when I walk as I did before, and see visual images, all related to my blessed life shared with Rochester. These and my walks will help me to live in the present moment with him and not project fear into a future I am not even guaranteed.

We can be hit by many strange physical symptoms when we grieve and experience deep loss. Others often have an entire list of symptoms and aches and pains.

I believe I have to begin regular walking again around our property and through the woods, something I had ceased to do when March 8th made its appearance. Too, there was still snow here in March and April and that curtailed walking then and set a pattern obviously for only the necessary, but none at all in the form of exercise. The healing power of walking reveals itself most dramatically in time of emotional crisis.

I had even written about the importance of walking in my previous book on prayer, and now my grief has caused me to neglect it. I have to keep *"walking"* through the pain and taking *"a stand,"* that our grieving for our animal companions and humans is essential, and to remember that *"No one can make you feel inferior without your consent."* Eleanor Roosevelt said that. It is on a tiny plaque on my desk and it has been a maxim for me for years. Rochester often patted the little plaque around my desk with his soft paw, reminding me of its importance.

On our walks I will take Rochester. You too can take your beloved animal companion if he is still on earth, or take him in spirit as I will do. When you were a child your imagination freely took flight. Be that child again and take along an animal of your choosing if you have no animal companion here or in Heaven. It can be your totem animal if you know it—or any animal you choose. Pray first, and believe then he was sent to you. Let the animal that first came to you in a burst of insight go along on your walks. This animal that suddenly appeared to you wants to walk with you just as Rochester will with me. The author of the quotation that opens this journal entry suggests the idea of your totem animal as companion in walking. She states that in many cultures it is believed that a totem animal is a natural connection between the animal and to whom it appears. I believe it can be your beloved animal companion if you have one, or one still not known to you. It can be a small animal, a large animal, a wild one, the first one that popped into your mind. Try to enjoy your walk in this way. Be open to letting this play of imagination lighten your spirit and connect you to nature. See what you can learn from the strange animal or your very own companion. Rochester has always taught me new things and will again on these walks. And I will write it all down in my Journal.

We often need a "*jog*" to our wounded minds and memories to help us remember to take care of ourselves when we grieve. There is no incentive to take care of myself at this time, but since I seem to have been given these sudden insights on my cramped legs, I will obey. Today I will begin my walks again, "*prayer walks*" as I used to call them. Now they will be "*memory walks*" as I carry Rochester within while taking every step, and also imagine him by my side walking. I have to remain invincible to complete our Journal, and to see that it gets out into the world to help others in their grief. I have to give others and myself *strong legs* to stand on. Rochester is seeing that I do just this. I want to one day reach *la Sainte Terre* to be with Rochester in Heaven.

Take a stroll with your soul.

—Linus Mundy

The healing power of walking reveals itself most dramatically in times of emotional crisis…. Nature facilitates communication with inner wisdom and higher powers.

—Carolyn Scott Kortge

Everywhere

He had ceased to meet us in particular places
in order to meet us everywhere.

—C.S. Lewis

Friday, June 21, 2002

THE LOVE I SHARED AND STILL SHARE FOREVER with Rochester is a gift. I carry this grief gladly, for without it would mean I had never had Rochester in my life. It is a gift from our one life lived together. I cannot ever comprehend life without Rochester, and I would not trade one moment of this sorrow, even with all the pain, in contrast to never having lived and loved with Rochester. It was a spiritual dimension of living that defies explanation, and now it continues on still yet another plane until we are together in Heaven. Without Rochester I cannot imagine what the past almost sixteen years would have been.

Perhaps there are some who have lost human or animal companion loved ones who wonder where their loved ones are. Please pray and find a peace in the certainty that they live on. I am secure in my belief of sharing life with Rochester in Heaven, and that my Dad is caring for him until I join them. Yet I know too, as many do, that my loved one is still *here* with me, for I experience him and sense him. His spirit never deserts me, never departs. He is around me, beside me, within me, and slumbers on my legs. This will always be so. It is an unfathomable comfort. It is a solace beyond words.

Losing my loved one's physical presence changed me. I see the world differently, and a sense of solid individualism has strengthened me. I do not have to answer to others about my grief. I am changed internally, spiritually, and in mysterious ways. There is a new person within that has stronger beliefs and an endurance level I did not know was ever possible. I believe Rochester's Anima, his breath and soul within me, his eternal gift to me, is this underlying strength. And yes, God's grace, and His Holy Spirit bestowed on me at conception. I have resources and power within me that rise up and sustain even in my most anguished moments of depletion, and of experiencing Rochester's physical absence. I believe it is my most devastating loss, yet I know it is imparting a wisdom to carry me through what days of my life I have left until I am in Heaven with Rochester. The life we had together cannot be duplicated. It was and is a divine gift. Both Rochester and I are transformed. You who read may come to know this transformation too, if you are deeply grieving for one who was and is a special world unto itself for you alone.

EVERYWHERE

He is near
My little dear—
He is far
He is my Star.

He is without
He is within—
In the silence
In the din.

He sustains
He ordains—
Removes fear
He is here.

For eternal   JGK
Rochester

Another Friday. Another Holy Hour from 5 to 6 PM in solitude, remembrance, prayer, tears, and eternal love. He is here.

The life we had together cannot be duplicated.
It was and is a divine gift.

Rochester on the cover of the book he inspired—
as well as the lifestyle of vegetarianism.

Forever

FOREVER

I leave in this doorway a rock—
Cracked open and broken as I—
And I cry and stand in shock—
That I am here to sanctify—

The place where we first met—
Where you patiently waited for me—
Now eyes tear-filled, cheeks wet—
And my heart in agony—

I thank God for your precious existence—
And leave the rock as a symbol you stand—
Forever in my life—pure magnificence,
So Holy and glorious and grand.

For my   JGK
beloved Rochester   June 23, 2002

Sunday, June 23, 2002

*I*T IS SUNDAY, JUNE 23RD. Our daughter Barbara is here from Pennsylvania to spend twelve days with us. It is a very difficult day for me for it is sixteen years ago this day that I adopted Rochester. In my

189

meditation of Tuesday, March 12th I have written in detail of how Rochester entered my life, and now it is the anniversary of that day. It was such a joyful day in 1986. I thought I was dreaming that I should have such a precious little being become mine. I never thought out life together could end.

On this day in the very early morning before light I dream of Rochester. His dear face and upper body are very clear but his lower body is partially covered by a barrier of some sort, perhaps a wooden partition. This is not clear, only my Rochester looking at me with his golden eyes and in great love is so very clear, and leaves of trees behind him. I cry in the dark as I waken both in joy because he appears to me, and too that the dream is over. But it comes as a gift from Rochester on this special day in our lives.

And so this morning after Mass and my many prayers at church concerning all the memories and meanings of this day, Bob, Barbara and I decide to have breakfast out in a new diner that has opened in Rochester. We are so happy Barbie is with us and I am so sad that Rochester is not. As I have planned for weeks, we drive to the nearby mall to the place where I adopted Rochester. The original small mall that I had once entered and found my beloved Rochester on a bench in a carton next to a man, is now a building with numerous offices within. I go to a door that would be nearest to the spot inside where I first encountered my little beloved. Bob pulls the car away from where I am so I may have privacy. It is overwhelming to be here and I fall apart. Over the years since I adopted him, each and every time we entered the town of Rochester, or shopped in that mall, or rode by it on the highway, I offered up prayers of thanksgiving to God for allowing this precious little one in my life. I never failed to do these things.

When in the mall I would go to the bench if empty, and lay my hands upon it, and thank God for Chester. If someone was sitting there I would stand to the side and pray. My gratitude for Rochester was ever alive and still is. I do the same now this Sunday. I pray and pray in thanksgiving for Rochester, and tell God and Rochester once again I am broken hearted but so appreciative he is ever mine and I am his.

Before I turn to go I look for the correct spot to leave a rock that I selected from our grassy yard before Mass. It is a rock broken and cracked open like my heart and from a spot beneath the shelf on our porch where

Rochester loved to sit. He viewed his world filled with the beauty of nature from this shelf. I knew his precious eyes had seen this rock in the grass below his perch. I dig it from the earth and take it with me and keep it in my pocket while in church and having breakfast. Now I place it on a cement foundation that runs the length of the base of the building as a trim. There is no other place to leave it. With more prayer I tell Rochester again that he is like a rock in my life, but like this chosen rock I am broken and shattered. He already knows and continually sends me such comfort. I feel the rock has more chance of remaining there indefinitely than if I take a bouquet of flowers. I am continually planting flowers in my gardens for him opposite the screened in porch and his personal shelf within. And so I leave the doorway in tears, an area that I once left with a carton sixteen years earlier containing the deepest of joy in the form of a precious marmalade and white kitten, my feline soulmate. The rest of the day fills with memories of all the 23rd of June held in 1986 as dear little Rochester and I began our blessed life together. And his Hibiscus plant blooms with a brand new coral blossom in his honor and memory.

1986

Today I journey back in years—
To a town not far away.
I fill with yearning and with tears—
Thinking of that joyous day.

For Rochester   JGK
June 23, 2002

Gift of Tears

Why, who makes much of a miracle? Not me!
I know nothing else but miracles!

—Walt Whitman

Grief is a spiritual death while still alive.

—Unknown

Monday, June 24, 2002

SINCE ROCHESTER'S PASSING it has been fifteen weeks and three days, and yet it always seems in the present. My heart is shattered and pieced together with the eternal love we share, but time seems to be existing as if it all just happened. The pain is intense and does not diminish, and my tears flow as if I am living in the moment of Chester being in my arms, and in the hours and weekend that followed. I live in the present of that pain and find it difficult to believe time has passed. Although I ache to hold him I cannot believe it has been fifteen weeks, for I could never exist without Rochester for even a day, and it would be an impossibility for *fifteen weeks and three days!* Therefore I am living in a dimension that exists outside of reality.

It has come to me that I have been given the *Gift of Tears* from God—and through these tears and in this dimension of time standing still, I can live an existence in a much closer spiritual proximity to Rochester. If I am willing to live as if he has just left physically, and be willing to endure in this passage of tears—I have been given a gift of both the deepest and highest magnitude! For then we shall remain on the edges and brinks of two worlds and exist in a oneness and closeness that is of supernatural origin and dimension.

But it requires the *Gift of Tears* that will be ever present as in the depth of grief when first he left physically. But that is how I have been existing! I feel I am being shown it is a *gift* if I am strong enough to accept it. Perhaps that is why it has continued to exist so as to give me time— and the true realization of what I will be experiencing if it continues and I choose it. I do choose it and accept it at this very moment, God, with all my broken heart, so that I may live in as deep an existence and dimension with my beloved little feline soulmate as possible until I join him in Heaven. Thank you, dear God, for this priceless gift.

GIFT OF GRACE AND TEARS

Between two worlds
I reside—
And I confide
it is surreal.
I cannot ever
lose my place—
For it's a grace,
a heavenly seal.
And with it
there are tears—
For years,
and years and years.

And though apart—
We live as one.
I the shadow
He the sun.

For beloved little   JGK
Rochester   June 2002

how fortunate we are you and i, whose home is timelessness.

—e.e. cummings

The memory — has never dimmed, nor has the pain of losing her diminished to any great degree. I have never wanted the pain of her loss to vanish. I have learned to live with it, and if there were no heartache left I honestly would have to confess that there was something seriously lacking in me—

—Dale Evans Rogers, *Angel Unaware*

Seek not to know Love's full extent,
For Death, not life, must measure Love—

— W.H. Davies

ROCHESTER

R eflective and rare
O verwhelmingly patient and precious—
C ompassionate, constant, contemplative and cherished.
H onorable, humble, beloved friend—
E nlightened and empowering encourager—
S acred, sagacious supporter—
T ender and thoughtful confidant
E minent and everlasting Angel
R ochester, renowned, radiant, remarkable companion.

Written to honor him and   JGK
in thanksgiving for the day   June 2000
he came into my life.

HARRY

H arry, handsome, honest helper—
A lso known as
R ochester
R eassuring soulmate—
Y ielding, loving advocate.

JGK
June 2000

Afterword

If you live to be a hundred,
I want to live to be
a hundred minus one day,
so I never have to live
without you.

—*Winnie the Pooh*

Friday, July 5, 2002

On February 12, 2002, just a little less than a month before Rochester entered Heaven, I wrote the above verse in my journal. It was like a prayer to me. Under it I wrote that it was for my Rochester and Bob. I also entered two other quotations that touched my heart that I will share soon. Obviously the wish in the above verse did not come to be though I live with Rochester deeply in spirit. But it breaks me apart to read that little poem. He was right by my side when I entered it in my journal. He is still by my side, though it is seventeen weeks this day that he was last visibly there. Oh, how can that be?

John Russell Lowell has written that "*All God's Angels Come to Us Disguised*" and they are often in the form of animals. In *Journal of Love* I have explored this. So many accounts in recent years are written about in animal books, other books I own, and in a magazine about Angels published by Guide Posts. Many times God has sent a loving animal when needed, sometimes for the animal's life time or sometimes momentarily

196

to rescue someone. Rochester came to me at a very difficult time of my life when, in despair, I did not value my life and asked God to take it. Two weeks later God set Rochester down in a small mall in a carton held by a father with two children sitting on a round bench outside a supermarket. He was holding a sign that read *"Free Kittens,"* and in divine intervention God brought us together.

Rochester has been an Angel and Guardian in so many difficult situations and all are recorded either in my previous books or my journals. God knows that at times a human needs a beloved animal angel companion to hold and care for and to be blessed with in continual presence, ministering healing that only an angel animal can minister

As I have written I believe too, that others who are open and want to be extremely close to their animal friends can achieve communication. I know there are countless humans in this world who communicate with animals and can do wondrous things on their behalf, and also this can greatly benefit the human involved. I would not want to live without this ongoing amazing communication that I still experience regularly in the time since March 8th.

Rochester became my feline soulmate and teacher and constant companion. Beside leading us to practice Ahimsa and become vegetarians for the animals' sake, he inspired all my books and countless poems. And my journals since 1986 contain continual reference to him as we shared our days and nights.

In *Compassion* I wrote that there is a beautiful quotation by an unknown author that has come to mind again and again since my precious Rochester became my inseparable companion. Everything I read seemed to have more meaning to me since Rochester entered my life. This quotation speaks of the little one I love. It also appears at the beginning of the Journal entry of Tuesday, March 12th, 2002

> *God never loved me in so sweet a way before. 'Tis He alone who can such blessings send. And when His love would new expressions find, He brought thee to me and He said—Behold a friend.*

I cannot read that without crying. If only I could have all those years over again with him. Please cherish your animal companions. I always cherished Rochester. He was and is my little love. Always cherish them and do not take your time with them for granted. I never did! Never brush them away in impatience. I never did! Never! I felt blessed! I love him so much and each moment with him was a gift. I would not even make Rochester move from my lap if he had fallen deeply asleep on me. I would wait until he woke naturally. He turned my existence upside down and taught me so much. He was and is pure love. I see with new spiritual eyes because he came into my life forever.

He gave light and love to personal letters I sent out. Photos I constantly took of him have touched many hearts including my own, and he appeared in the 1996 Humane Society's Desk Calender on Thanksgiving Day, November 28, when his photo was selected from 20,000 entries. This same page from the calendar appeared in my book *Compassion*. I believe his loving image gave joy to all who saw him. Too, our Christmas Cards are often photos I take of the beauty here in the woods that surrounds us. This past Christmas we sent out a handsome card created by Bob with Rochester's picture on it. We had never done that before, and I wanted him to be on our cards this time. How grateful I am I was inspired to suggest that, and Bob created the card with Rochester's picture and a loving message. I am still sending photos out of him too in almost every personal note and letter I write. Bob makes beautiful writing paper for me with his various pictures on now and long before he left. There are framed photos of him in various rooms of our cottage as well. I have countless photos of him that I took through the years ever since he was a kitten. I always had my camera with us daily. Please, always take pictures of your precious companions be they animal or human, or you will so deeply regret it if they should leave you. I took pictures of Bob and my six children and our three Cairn Terriers through the years, so I began immediately with capturing Rochester on film. So many precious pictures of him! Some are in all my books. These pictures are a gift of extraordinary worth to me now until the day I die. Please, always take pictures. When a roll of developed film would come back in the mail and the majority were of Chester, Bob would often say, *"Don't you have enough pictures of him now?"* He knew my answer before he asked. I am so thankful I followed my heart. Chester constantly looked so adorable to me, and did things that moved me and were out of the ordinary—and I have now all those priceless moments together to hold forever in my heart and hands, and see again and again with eyes that once beheld him in life.

I pray each night before sleep that he comes to me in a dream or that I see him in our cottage. In an older journal I have recorded:

Animals may aid us in our everyday lives, in our dreams, meditations. Since they were created before humans they are closer to The Source and can act as allies, guides and familiars in our search for wholeness.

—an Inuit woman

All of these times with him in dreams and sightings have blessed me beyond words capable of expressing it these past weeks and months.

It is written:

With the first dream that comes with the first sleep I run, I run, I am gathered to thy heart.

—A. Meyzell (1850-1922)

Our subconscious mind knows things our conscious mind does not. I believe our loved ones in Heaven try to communicate through our dreams, and I have heard this stated by others who are spiritually knowledgeable and believe this too.

Author G. Scott Sparrow has expressed:

It is written that it is probably true that most give waking visions more credence than dreams. However, dreams have not always been considered less real or meaningful than waking experiences or so-called waking visions.

Writer Morton Kelsey states that his analysis of both Old and New Testaments reveals that dreams and visions, or rather the singular concept of the dream-vision, occupies a central place in the Judeo-Christian tradition. Kelsey points out that the ancient position was to regard the dream as *the state in which a vision naturally occurred.* According to this view the vision is the content of the dream. He makes the point that the vision can intrude upon waking awareness, and the dream was considered the natural state in which visions were experienced.

It is written that Kelsey is fond of displaying a Bible from which all references to dreams and visions have been removed. There is simply not much left. Early Church fathers believed that dreams originated from different levels of the soul.

Just today I heard it spoken that if there is agitation and upset and past issues in your dreams concerning your loved one, that dream is given so that these things may be worked on and solved by *you*, perhaps through prayer and asking forgiveness if this is necessary.

But if the dream with your loved one in is all love and extremely comforting, and your loved one is attempting to show you loving things and times and moments shared together, *it is your loved one!* It truly is! Then this is a gift!

My dreams of Rochester have been loving and comforting gifts, pure blessings. All of these times with him in dreams and sightings have blessed me beyond words capable of expression these past weeks and months.

Be open to your prayers being heard, and to experiencing what ever is given you, and you may be surprised as was I. These are gifts and they sustain, and no matter what our religion or church affiliation, we have a personal relationship with God, and it is written in scripture that *all good and perfect gifts come down from the Father of Lights.* (James 1:17) It does not say you have to belong to a certain Church, Synagogue or Mosque or any place of worship, before you receive blessings from God. We can go directly to Him in prayer. My heart was broken forever when Rochester was not physically healed and his physical presence left me. I felt abandoned by God for He knows how deeply I love Him and love Rochester. But abandonment is not truth. One day I will understand when I join Rochester, and always I continue to pray and thank God for Rochester.

He was so precious and did such loving little things. Whenever I mouthed emphatically but silently, *"I love you, Chester,"* his eyes would brighten and get larger than usual, and he would come very close to my face with his front paws on my chest or neck so he could be up close and personal. He would bump his little forehead into mine (a feline kiss) and wait for me to repeat the words. We then would repeat our little ritual. He could not get close enough to me when I told him my love in that way. He always did this before settling down to sleep on me too.

Blinking our eyes across the room at each other slowly and deliberately is also a feline kiss that says *"I love you"* and was worthy of a poem written for him. We did that often also. We did not keep our love a secret, for we also communicated and still communicate soul to soul, mind to mind and I record all of these precious interchanges. I have written about this communication in my *Journal of Love* and in this present journal and other books. Those we love who are in Heaven, animals or humans, can be conversed with, or I certainly converse with my human loved ones. I do not receive messages as I do from Rochester. Often a picture will appear in my mind however. Too, I have significant dreams in their regard, often in relation to what I have talked to them about. But the dream may not come immediately, but often weeks later. My communication with Chester is unique, alive and of God. Nothing has ever been like what I have been experiencing with Rochester in communication, for we are so close and our love is so precious and eternal and created by God. I will never forget inhaling his sweetness and good nature and never ending love when I would push my nose into his soft fur. I treasure those moments forever. I often press his dear fur I trimmed from him on March 8th to my face. How grateful I am to have this.

And every morning and night I forgive everyone that is in my life or ever has been (God knows them all), and I forgive myself. I am intent upon doing this, for Rochester has caused great changes, and nothing in my past that was painful, and there have been many such things, can ever compare to the utter depleting pain I am experiencing these past months. I cannot ever risk not being with Rochester in Heaven because I cannot forgive. *I can forgive and I do!* I ask God to also forgive me for any pain I have ever, knowingly or unknowingly, caused anyone, even though I have been doing this for years! Perhaps it is sufficient to do it all only once, but I am compelled to do it repeatedly and ever shall. My eternal hope and belief is to spend eternity with Rochester who awaits.

It is difficult to continually focus on life and living and on Rochester's precious life, rather than his passing, when I mourn so. When you love deeply and forever and physically lose that someone, you go back and forth constantly from life here to eternity, from the world you are living in to life with that loved one in spirit. My grief is so Holy. I know others feel this too who grieve. Grief is on-going for each of us at some time or other. If we dearly, dearly loved our precious one, each will deal with this grief differently. Fear of death is forever removed when you know loved ones await you in Heaven.

Rochester has always been such a spiritual presence in my life. Though I have explained the *"Harry"* of his name given him by Bob, I have not made reference to the name *"Whittier."* That is a little more unusual to write about. It is a name I gave to him when I dedicated him to God with prayers from my heart and sprinkled him with Holy Water on Easter Eve when he was two years old. Rochester is a sacramental and always has been to me. He is a sentient being with a soul, as are all God's creatures, and I felt the necessity to privately do this. I shared this for the first time in my *Journal of Love* and feel I would like to share it also in this journal. Before that only my husband Bob knew.

Perhaps there are others reading this who may wish to consider it for your beloved animal companions. I chose the name *Whittier* because I daily enjoy reading and writing poetry and named him after John Greenleaf Whittier who lived in Massachusetts but who spent much of his life in New Hampshire, very especially summers. Also Whittier wrote his famous poem containing the line *"Barefoot boy with cheek of tan"* and this line describes Rochester. Too we live near Mount Whittier, and Rochester was born in New Hampshire—therefore, this name seemed appropriate and dignified for all these reasons. Four years later on his birthday this was the subject of a poem I wrote for him to commemorate the day.

BLESSINGS ON THEE

A fine New Hampshire poet wrote
These dear lines I love to quote.
"Blessings on thee little man—
Barefoot boy with cheek of tan."

I give these blessings to my "boy"—
Whose sweet existence brings such joy.
In love—He's called my "little man"
And I kiss his cheeks of tan.

Around the house he loves to pad—
Barefoot—just like any lad!

This fond old poem to him applies.
My heart and soul it gratifies.
For this "little man" that's mine—
Is loving, precious—and feline!

(Whittier is his spiritual name.
For Poet and Mountain of great fame.)

Dedicated to   JGK
Rochester Harry Whittier Kolb   May 30, 1991
on his birthday—May 30, 1991   New Hampshire
(born in New Hampshire)

I wanted to be as spiritually close to Rochester as possible, so I truly paid great attention to his expressions and actions and his personal way with me. I tried to act when I felt he was showing me something that required a response, and I let him lead me to other rooms in order for him to show me what he had in mind also. I respected greatly his attempts at communication, and as a result I learned so many dear aspects of Rochester and his teachings. I felt we had extraordinary communication as time passed. The fact that he wanted us to be bonded immediately and initiated the entire ritual was a sacred gift from him to me. I always treated him with great love and dignity and still do, but I would have even if that ritual had not taken place. I had fallen in love with this priceless little kitten, a kitten I had longed to have since I was twenty-one. I believe the Angels have helped us to communicate for it was an Angel who encouraged me to use writing in communication with him. As I shared in *Journal of Love,* one day Rochester gave me a great encouragement in regard to doubt — one of many, but this one was dealing with it in a way I needed to hear that particular hour. He spoke to my mind and heart and I wrote:

Do not ever doubt that these words are mine, for if you do, you are taking credit for what is mine and this is not your nature. You believe in me and so never let doubt creep in. You know I am capable of this, but when you begin to reflect on what others may think, then you may doubt this precious experience. Believe, for I am writing to you—or letting you write to me. Such a partnership and bond and love we have, My Love. (He called me that "love name" always.)

How can I ever doubt these messages I continue to receive? He lives in spirit with me, his Anima is within me, and his dear being is in Heaven. His messages are indeed valid! I could never doubt! Perhaps our learning this communication was all preparation to help us spiritually now, as well as when he was physically with me. Never doubt that you and your beloved animal companions can communicate, on earth or when they have physically left. Take the time right now if you have even a flicker or inkling of belief, before it is too late. Cherish your animal by still yet another dimension of living with him in his love. God and Mary and the Angels will help you. I have shared much in *Journal of Love* of communications Bob and I received from the Holy Spirit, music and hymns, that we value as God-given gifts. Also messages of Angelic nature, and so I could never doubt what Rochester and I were given and I am eternally grateful for it. Please pray about this and consider all I have shared so you can be as deeply one with your dear animal companions as possible. It is pure gift forever and sustains in deepest grief.

Years ago when Chester was younger I discovered a display of name cards in a bookstore with the meaning of each name on the individual card and a scripture verse. They were parchment like in color, about two inches by three inches plasticized. I framed one for my desk and carried another in my wallet. Chester's name meant "fortified camp." Indeed, along with being my Angel and Star and many more wondrous things, he was my "fortified camp." His presence and essence and unconditional love gave me inner strength I often did not realize I had in the face of some terrible trials and fears in life. His mere entrance into my life at one of those difficult periods proved this and he remained my spiritual protector and always will be.

Today in *Bartlett's Familiar Quotations* when looking for a quotation, I came upon this little poem totally unfamiliar to me though the poet is not. It struck me immediately that it spoke in a sense of Rochester's on-going words to me also—*quaint and beautiful* and *many lustred,* and *coloured* with love. But *his* words are stored in my heart, yet too written in my journals and *put upon a shelf,* ready to take down and read at a moment's notice. Too, they continue to be received and recorded in journals regularly.

> *My words are little jars*
> *For you to take and put upon a shelf.*
> *Their shapes are quaint and beautiful,*
> *And they have many pleasant colours and lustres*
> *To recommend them.*
>
> —Amy Lowell

His words are not all that I store away. His little carrier that he travelled in thousands of miles from June 1986 to January 1996 and only occasionally in for check-ups after that locally, is going to be a carrier of his keepsakes when I finish this journal. I will keep all his toys in there, some already are there. And too, any birthday cards from him that Bob "helped" him to write to me and just all things personal. There are many. Originally I was going to place all the letters of caring and sympathy that we received following March 8th, but I think now they will have a separate lovely container. I will put only things in his carrier that applied to his life and our glorious days of living together. The carrier will have a special spot in my writing room. He never cared for it much yet was always content in the carrier. We had to plan ahead to get him into it. Once on the road he was basically happy and was a dear little traveller, usually 430 miles at one time. I always kept my hand or forearm in it with him. He liked to hold onto me. I will not wipe it out but want his scent within—the loveliest of scents. I still bury my face in his wildlife quilt each night where his beloved scent still remains, after I finish writing when I kneel beside the bed to pray. His flowered tin with his ashes sits next to the quilt all day and is carried downstairs with me in the evening. Then at bed time it sits on the table next to me. These rituals remain and always shall, and sustain.

We have had no mice since Chester went to Heaven. Not one! If you could only know how unusual this is for a cottage in the woods. The mouse he caught and we released the Tuesday night of his last week, was the last mouse. It would seem his spirit presence is caring for us in many ways.

And the two crows still come daily to our deck and feeders and they are Holy to me. We have an abundance of birds this year like no other time. There are even more Mallards not just "Mr. and Mrs." I know why all these things occur. Each Sunday here at home we continue to have a private little spiritual service for him using our own original prayers and meditations. Often at Mass I sit in tears. Music there, on TV, or anywhere can suddenly overwhelm. His sweet Christmas stocking bearing the image in needle point of a marmalade and white cat shall always be hung on Christmas Eve as in years past.

And when we return from Mass, the Post Office or anywhere we have been, as we approach our door I await to hear his little paws come walking across the piano keys just inside as he greets us. And always once inside I go immediately to our bedroom where I know in spirit he has run ahead of me and is waiting on the bed. We share moments alone in joy for I know he is there. Centuries ago Paracelsus said, *"Absence of evidence is not evidence of absence."* The unseen can represent valid evidence and what we know to be true in our hearts can not be shaken by unbelievers!

I do not know if I recorded it elsewhere in this journal though I had great intention to do so for it is a miracle, but each day and night since March 8th I have experienced Rochester in a blessed way. Even if I have written this previously that is fine, for I write it then now to tell you that it has continued and never stopped. I have been told in my heart and soul it never shall.

ALWAYS THERE

Upon my legs
    you sleep each night—
And though your body's
    out of sight—
You impart warmth
    and heat intense—

Our one heart burns—
    with love immense.

Within our heart
    I kneel and bow—
For your eternal
    presence and vow—
And lie awake
    in awe and prayer—
Thanking God
    you slumber there.

For beloved   JGK
Rochester   May 2002

At night he sleeps upon my legs as always and I feel enormous heat, more than when he was physically there. If I wake in the night it is ever present. I never move just as I never moved him from my lap when he was physically here. It happens when I sit on the sofa too, legs stretched down the length as I did when he was here in body and wanted to lie on me. I still put the bathrobe on my legs that he enjoyed and continues to enjoy. When he is on my lap after I have dressed we especially had a little ritual when I first came into the living room early each morning that continues. My lap fills with the heat of his spiritual presence. I am so blessed, so grateful! I pray for and am open to any sign; visual, or the heat of his presence, or sounds that declare his being here with me, though I know he shall ever be with me if there were no signs ever! Of that I am certain! Yesterday when alone and writing this journal on the screened in porch I heard the familiar tinkle of his tags against his plate on his feeding table. Not once, but twice, and enough to make me put all papers aside and walk softly to the door of the kitchen that adjoins the porch. He was not visually there, yet there is no explanation for that sound of his tags that I know so well and heard for years. But he was there! He is here! And I thank God for the gift of Rochester in all spiritual dimensions forever.

There are so many more incidents and happenings in our life together that I can share, but perhaps it is time to let you reflect upon all you have read in this journal. It was written not only for my broken heart but for others that are heartbroken too because of the passing of a loved one, be they animal or human.

I believe an aspect of my grief, in addition to the precious one of "*The Gift of Tears,*" is so I may always have deep understanding for others in their grief, and try to help them even if from afar, yet never interfere. Often sincere and faithful prayer over an extended period is all that can be done. I experience grief of other authors I mentioned merely through their written words. I feel empathy and inner devastation for and with them. Always I have tried to help others in their grief in the past, and too more recently, because of grief of another sort I personally experienced. Often my main role has merely been as a listener, to just "be there" for another in pain. People often just need to be listened to, not fixed. There are times you cannot tread where you may be an intrusion to someone's heartbreak. There is a fine line you may not cross, for unwelcome words or presence of someone not in deep understanding of the pain being experienced, can only increase the anguish.

My grief for Rochester is akin to a living, throbbing entity unto itself. I have attempted to write it in this journal so that others who need a companion through this passage can have one in the quietness and silence of reading these entries on these pages while alone. You can always put it aside if it is not in compliance with your grief.

There is a quotation I have shared previously that speaks too of what I have tried to do in writing Rochester's and my life story, or love story. It states;

> *The stories people tell have a way of taking care of them. If stories come to you, care for them. And learn to give them away where they are needed. Sometimes a person needs a story more than food to stay alive. That is why we put these stories in each others' memory. This is how people care for themselves.*
>
> —Barry Lopez, *Crow and Weasel*

Telling our story is helping to care for Rochester and me, and I pray it will help others also, just as other stories help me.

Perhaps many who read still have their beloved ones with them on earth as I did Rochester when I first read *Maya's First Rose* and *The Best*

Cat Ever. This journal is not to make you sad or have tears, though perhaps that will happen as it did when I read the beautiful books I just mentioned. It is meant to make you realize the incredible gift you have in the life of your dear cat or dog or other animal, and to never take your days and years together for granted. To ignore your precious animal would be comparable to not accepting and opening a gift from God! Live in the sacrament of the moment and cherish each one with your beloved. Begin to live in that way now. That is Rochester's and my gift to you, the writings in this journal of ours that tell of our never ending love, the love we lived out our entire life together before March 8th, and in the days since, and will in all the days we have left before we are together in Heaven.

God Bless You.

I also have to say that you have experienced a wonderful, close, and loving relationship, and a richness and satisfaction you may never experience in a relationship with another human being. The happy relationships we share with our pets are the jewels in our lives. All the material possessions in the world cannot equal this joy.

—Sonya Fitzpatrick, *What the Animals Tell Me*

We must have loved each other
long before this life,
for when I first saw you
my heart leapt for joy.

—inspired by Poetry of India

In all these weeks since Rochester left I have not been able to play our special nighttime music on the tape recorder on the headboard. I have so many tears within and visibly over normal everyday living once shared with Rochester when he was here in body in all his love and gentleness and goodness, that I am afraid to push the button of that recorder. To be without this music since March 8th is unreal, having had it nightly in our lives since 1989. Perhaps I am inflicting unnecessary punishment upon myself. Perhaps as always in the past it will be our healing music. I have again made an intention that I hope to fulfill. I will play it by the time I finish writing this journal.

Though our nighttime music began with the ethereal and magical playing of Mike Rowland's "*The Fairy Ring*" those many years ago that Rochester and I love and share, in the past several years before I played it, I recited a lovely prayer aloud for Bob, Rochester and myself. This was in addition to our own silent prayers and my blessing Rochester's forehead with the *Sign of the Cross*.

It is a new prayer Bob wrote for us several years ago adapted from an old one we recited as children, and far more comforting. I have included it in each of my books except the first, and will again now in this one for you.

As we lay down to sleep this night
Please keep us safe 'til morning light.
Grant us sleep and needed rest
And fill our dreams with happiness.
For Lord we know that with you near
There's nothing that we have to fear.
Guide us where you want to lead
And be with those we love and need.

In the past two years Bob has written music for it and recorded it on his electronic keyboard on a separate tape. At times he sings on it also. It is now this music I always played first at night for the three of us, as Bob falls asleep quickly. Then "*The Fairy Ring*" was for Rochester and me. He and I always boarded the strains to enter "*The Ring*" together—and eventually make that journey to sleep and dream. And we shall make that journey again forevermore.

See! I will not forget you. I have carved you on the palm of my hand
—Isaiah 49:15

And in the palm of my hand rests his soft little white paws.

My Angel and Star

Rochester enjoying the porch and
being safely outdoors in nature he loved.

I carry these words
with me all day until I can
spill them like stardust,
silver into the night—

I love you. I love you.
I love you.

                       —Unknown

My Angel and Star

Those who are wise shall shine like the brightness of the sky,
and those who lead many to righteousness, like the stars forever and ever.
—Daniel 12:3

Monday, July 8, 2002

THE SCRIPTURE ABOVE SPEAKS OF MY BELOVED ROCHESTER. Today it is four months since I last held him in my arms, last inhaled the sweetness of his fur and being, last kissed his dear face while in his earthly body. Writing poetry came into my life anew just as Rochester entered my life. I had not written any poems for a span of many years. Now I had a blessed little marmalade and white Angel in my life and poems began to arrive, and especially poems about him. He is my Angel and Star. He inspired hundreds of poems since 1986, many of which we have put into our books. So many, many of the poems were written for him alone and about him, and with such enormous love. The merest thing he would do I would capture in a poem. I am so thankful that I did. I am still writing them. The majority in the greater portion of this book are written since March 8th. I will always write poems for and with Rochester for he shall be my inspiration forever. I just look at a photograph of him or think a thought of him, which is constant, and poetic lines form in my mind.

I would like to share my entire collection of poems about Rochester with you but they would fill an entire book of their own. Instead I shall leave with you the following poems that speak of him as either a *"star"* or an *"angel,"* for he was both of these to me, and much, much more, and

212

both stars and angels are in Heaven as he is. I never dreamed he would ever be there without me. In a journal on February 12, 2002, the same day I entered the quotation by Winnie the Pooh in the beginning of the Afterword, I also entered this—

If you should die before me, ask if you could bring a friend.

—Unknown

Why was I entering such quotations? It was surely not because I ever thought we would be separated! I am certain it was because they spoke of the deep desire to forever be together and I just love Rochester so, I wrote down anything that eluded to our deep love. I also entered the same day for him:

Animals are really special; they are a piece of God. They're like Angels. They come into our lives and give nothing but joy.

—Fred Travalena

Yes, he was and is my Angel and Star and all wondrous things blessed and good. In my *Enchantment of Writing*, I wrote *"He is poetry to me; he is love, music, prayer, joy and consolation and so much more. He is my personal Angel and my inspiration!"*

I believe God allowed an Angel in my life in the precious form of my beloved Rochester. He has always shined his love upon me like a bright and glittering star, and I continually felt and continue to feel the warmth and glow of his love and light in all areas of my life. I reaffirm as I did earlier, I am a finer and better person because of my dear, sweet Angel and Star.

Trying to put love into words is like trying to catch the stars, hold sunlight in a basket, or make a rainbow last forever.

—Unknown

Though some of these poems have been included in previous books of ours, I wish to include in this new *Journal of Love* written to honor him, this small collection of poetry written during our blessed life on earth together as one. We shall always be one. It is written:

Poetry is simply the most beautiful, impressive, and widely effective mode of saying things.

—Matthew Arnold

I know too, that Rochester is truly a healer to me. All through the years he brought healing to me in varied forms. He never left me when I was ill or sad. At times it was unreal and so deeply moving, the length of time he would stay upon my lap and minister to me. He is still ministering to me and always shall.

I begin this small poetry collection that is dedicated to him with a poem telling of his devotedness and deep love that forever continues. I too, tenderly and devotedly love him forevermore.

HEALER

Often when I am sad,
            concerned or ill—
He'll clasp both paws around my hands
            with a will
To make me right.
            And soon will come light.

He'll never leave my lap—
            nor ever nap.
Long hours shall pass
            he'll hold me fast—
For he is there to heal—
            and it is precious and surreal.

He is God's Angel, in disguise—
            —a joy forever—my divine surprise.

For Rochester   JGK
with love and gratitude   August 28, 1996

May these poems bless you, and may you always write your own poems as well to honor those you deeply love, be they animal or human. Poems can never be taken from you and will hold memories like time capsules hold treasures, and shall belong to you and your beloved one forever in God, just as you belong to each other, and as Rochester and I are one in Him.

> *Death frees the dead but*
> *not the living.*
> *You are gone—but are*
> *with me still.*
>
> —Unknown

EVER WITH ME

Four months have fled.
　　　You softly tread
Into my days.
　　　I feel the rays
My Star so dear.
　　　I know you're here.

I pick up pen
　　　Begin to write
And that is when
　　　You send your light—
And poems flow
　　　Through heart and head.
I daily know
　　　You are not dead.

Ever with me
　　　Angel muse.
Forever sending
　　　Your dear clues.

That though you're gone—
Invisibly—
With every dawn
You walk with me.

For my Angel and Star   JGK
Rochester   July 28, 2002

ANGEL OF LIGHT

Angel of light
    bright sacrosanct one
        that shone in my darkness
        and plight—

You radiated
    that dark night
        in the starkness
        of pain and tears—

And in embracing you
    in my arms
        and feeling your soft fur—
        your Angelic purr,

You banished my alarms
    and fears—
        instilling healing
        comfort and peace.

Tears cease—and
    stealing
        my heart anew
        you fill it with joy.

For beloved Rochester   JGK
                                        2000

UNDERSTANDING

I look at him this night
        realizing anew that I am seeing
           a being
                of light.
An Angel stretched down my legs—
        with tiny uplifted face—begs
           to commune, with sighs
                gently blinks his golden eyes.

Mind to mind, heart to heart—
        one soul.
Such secrets we impart!

His gentle paws now clasp my hand—
        sweetly console.
Nodding—he knows I understand.

To Rochester   JGK
with love   January 1999

A being of light
An Angel stretched
down my legs
JGK

His gentle paws
now clasp my hand.
(from poem "Understanding"
by JGK)

Drawing made of Rochester
after we communed and he
fell asleep holding my left hand
as I sketched. September 26, 1999

ANGELIC HOST

He sits upon my lap—gazing into my eyes—
All love—and fully aware I know his disguise
Revealed to me compassionately through the years—
In tender moments—or when I've needed breath—or been in tears.
And so when his gaze shifts to beyond my shoulder
And his eyes widen to become rounder and golder
In recognition, and he moves his stare slowly to the ceiling
Then climbs gently up my being in that direction—I should be kneeling!
For I am in the presence of Angels that have to me been shown—
Through his awe and reverence, and made known
By one who is one—and welcomes others here from day to day.
I feel their silent presence come our way.
And in this small room I sit in splendor—dumbfounded—
For by Angels I am daily surrounded.

I do not yet have his eyes to see.
I only know a feline Angel lives with me.

Dedicated to   JGK
Rochester—   November 4, 1995
and our Angels   New Hampshire

AN ANGEL'S TOUCH

We hold hands when we're alone.
This is only known
by one or two—
but I will tell you
That it is the most moving thing,
like the brush of an Angel's wing—
To feel that soft, small white paw—
feather-light with no hint of claw
Resting on my hand.
Only few can understand.

Then I place my other hand upon his paw—
  and it is the dearest phenomenon I ever saw—
For he then puts his other paw on me—
  (and I do not want to be free!)
And our little stack of love and affection
  at times brings tears—and reflection—
Upon our life together and moments captured
  for we two so alike—become enraptured
By the simplest things,
  —as paws brushing hands like Angels' wings.

Dedicated to Rochester   JGK
with great love   August 28, 1996
for the anniversary of the
day of his adoption (and mine)
June 23, 1986

GUARDIAN ANGEL

Little being filled with love—
You fit my heart just like a glove—
Revealing soul—in silent gaze—
And constant presence through the days.

Waiting in anticipation—
On bathrobed lap—your chosen station,
You remain—to underscore—
You long that I'll be strong once more.

Golden eyes in concentration
Search my eyes in adoration—
Little paws clasp firm my hand,
Telling me you understand.

Purring me to sleep and rest—
To make me well is your sweet quest.

Guardian Angel in soft fur—
White and marmalade comforter.

Dedicated to   JGK
  Rochester Harry Whittier Kolb   April 20, 1991
  (Chester)   New Hampshire

FELINE ANGEL—GOD'S GIFT

I have been yours now
For nine years, and I bow
To your wisdom, gentleness and caring—
For time and presence—allowing the baring
Of my soul into yours.
Our love and bond forever endures.

I look into golden eyes and see your soul -
And in fixed oneness—am made whole.
Your tender being rights all wrong—
And you are my eternal song.
With unconditional love that brings me healing—
You are Angel Guardian—ever revealing—
God.

In love and tribute to Rochester   JGK
for the anniversary of his adoption   September 8, 1995
June 23, 1995—and always   New Hampshire

ANGEL BEING

With all my soul I know that he—
Was sent from heaven just for me.
An angel in soft marmalade fur,
Large golden eyes—deep soothing purr.

He speaks to me without a word—
And yet each message I have heard.

The silence shared throughout the days—
Ministering in mysterious ways—
Ever with me—his small being—
Confirms it is Angel I am seeing!

Beneath my heart he sleeps each night—
And keeps it whole—warm with his light.
There is no need to see his wings—
Just seeing him—and my soul sings!

Written for Rochester—   JGK
in love and gratitude   February 28, 1994
for his being   New Hampshire

IN DISGUISE

Often an Angel comes in disguise,
With handsome face and luminous eyes.
That he's dressed in soft fur and appearing most wise,
Adds to the mystery of this spiritual surprise.

His white and marmalade coat has a radiance and glisten—
His steady gaze in my eyes tells me I am to listen.
The soft white paw on my hand is heavenly significance—
And I instantly succumb to his Angelic magnificence.

For dear Rochester   JGK
                                                 July 2001

More and more mankind will discover that we have to turn to poetry to interpret life for us, to console us, to sustain us.

Poetry is nothing less than the most perfect speech of man, that in which he comes nearest to being able to utter the truth.
—Matthew Arnold, *Essays in Criticism*

I would emphatically and tenderly add too, that writing and poetry have been and always shall be my way of reaffirming Rochester's blessed existence—and our oneness.

Wearing a purple bow—
taken on his first birthday, 1987

Postscript

My writing is a deepening need
And pen slips o'er the page with speed.
And oft when I look back to read—
I see God meant my soul to feed.

—JGK

Books are companions in grief.

—JGK

Friday, July 19, 2002

THERE ARE MANY THINGS WRITTEN ABOUT throughout this book that speak of what you may wish to do or what you may wish to keep if your beloved animal ever has his final day (may he never!). I believe I have shared deeply every aspect of my feelings regarding all these heart breaking matters, including cremation or burial. As I did with Maya's (Martin Scot Kosins) and Polar Bear's (Cleveland Amory) books, perhaps you will find comfort in rereading this one of mine from time to time. Even an unseen, unknown friend that truly understands your grief is more consoling than one who is present and known but does not understand. I know this for certain. The two authors I have just mentioned have especially helped me again and again, as did the books I bought for help March 18th—on my visit to the bookstore. I was also later sent a book by my daughter Laurel and one by my friend Joanne— each in a different religious tradition, Christian and Buddhist. These also

223

are moving and comforting. Brad and Sherry Steiger's thoughts are also mentioned in this journal from writings of theirs that comfort.

My daughter Jessica later gave me a book with "Chester" in the title though about a goose and not about a little cat. And my youngest daughter Janna sent me a lovely pale green hardback copy book to use as a journal (a type book I have used for years, and green is my favorite color). Inserted in the marbleized copy book on separate sheets were the answers to many questions posed at the end of chapters in my own book, The Enchantment of Writing. Her taking time to ponder these questions and reflections and write them down was her gift to me. She knew Rochester had been with me through the creating of them.

Chris, my friend at Blue Dolphin continues to send inspiring e-mail that has told of several additional visions of Rochester that have given me such enormous comfort. His insights into the mysteries of nature and his walks there, are kept all together to reread for inspiration and help. They are a spiritual book to me, with on-going additions.

More recently my friend Jeanne referred me to a book also containing many testimonies of bereavement for humans, one of which she has written, which I ordered on an internet bookstore but I have not as yet read. I have found anew how strongly and deeply I need books and that they are my friends. Strangely my own books I have written mentioned in this journal have helped me anew even though I cried and cried, for they all hold Rochester in the pages as I hold him in my heart and soul and once held him in my arms.

But most importantly I feel making the effort to go to the bookstore ten days after March 8th to buy my first books, forced me to look for help myself rather than depend on anyone. Drop your expectations. You, and others too, often learn there are not many to depend upon.

After perhaps an initial response to the passing of your loved one, and often not even that, you realize this is basically a corridor or passage you must travel alone. Others travelling this road before me have realized this, be it grief for animal companion or human, and authors Dominick Dunne, Martin Scot Kosins, and Cleveland Amory have revealed it as have other authors I have read during this period. You must rely on your own inner spiritual resources and on your self. And although you grieve so, you will discover an inner strength given by God, and given too, by your very own companion for whom you grieve.

I knew no books on grieving (for I always avoided them) aside from those I have mentioned, and I feel the ones I did buy that day found me and were lit up spiritually in some way to attract me. I know God and Rochester helped me. And I read and reread those books and continue to read them. I cannot move past reading on grief and the thoughts within those now known pages. They were like a life saver and an Angel as I was drowning in despair. I still need to read in those particular books bought that day of March 18th, and *Maya* and *The Best Cat Ever*. I just need them! I cannot read anything else—with the exception of one other that I began to reread in July. I have mentioned this book and author in my previous book, *Journal of Love*. The book is *What The Animals Tell Me—Developing Your Innate Telepathic Skills to Understand and Communicate with Your Pets* by Sonya Fitzpatrick. On June 3rd on the Animal Planet channel began a one-hour program that is on each week with Sonya communicating with both animals that are alive and too, that have passed on. She has never met the owners or animals before her first encounter with them. She brings great truths and solace to both—and affirms what I am experiencing and have written, that our animals that have passed on are ever with us and around us always. I watch it through tears and often great sobbing. It is such a consolation! I believe both her book and the program would help those in grief, but too it is for all who love animals. You would have to check your area listing for the time of her television program.

Therefore, I am not going to list the books I bought that day for if you are grieving too, then letting the right books find you will be part of your consolation. I cannot say healing. Each person is different. Simply go to a bookstore you like and plan to spend time. Going out to do this is part of your help. I did not want to leave our woods. Pray before you go and allow yourself to be shown what books are for you. It will happen. Take your time. The bookstore I went to that day I have always loved to go to since Rochester was a kitten. But that particular day of March 18th I was numb. There was no joy just tears, even while in the store. But you do need to go to a bookstore and you do need to read. Too, please buy yourself a journal while you are there, one that appeals to you in every way; size, feel of cover, texture of paper, lined or unlined pages, and color and design, if any, upon it. If one or more of these qualities are missing that would be essential to your being faithful in writing in it, then you will make excuses not to write. Truly pray and spend time in selecting your journal. The one I selected I described earlier is perfect for me, and for Rochester too. There is one waiting that is perfect for you too. A new pen also will help you to stay faithful in writing. My journal is written in green ink as are all since 1989. Green is Rochester's and my favorite color. I cannot emphasize the importance of writing. I wrote both this book beginning immediately after Rochester went to Heaven, and too have been writing in my new journal. Most entries are exactly as in this journal you are holding, others even much more deeply personal that I feel I cannot share. I will soon begin another journal identical to it. Please write. It will help you in your pain. It keeps me sane, and I am also creating testimonies to Rochester and our love and life together. Our loved ones are deserving of this, and our precious words to have forever will be everlastingly recorded to honor our dear ones. Please write. It is a deep and Holy act of love. Rochester also knows that. He is a writer too.

JUST FOR YOU

Flowers growing just for you
Are filling all my natural view.
With my hands and on my knees
I planted them, while summer breeze
Urged the blooms to sway and swing—
And all the while the birds on wing
Flew in to notice all the flowers—
And colored too those summer hours.

Your tall Hibiscus lush and green
Adds coral outbursts to the scene.
Blossoms now of every hue
Fill seven gardens just for you.

For dearest Rochester   JGK
                                                          July 28, 2002

Just as I have been writing poems as gifts to Rochester, our daughter Barbara gave me both the gift of her presence to lighten my heart, and a poem. She recently came from Pennsylvania to spend twelve days with us in the last weeks of June.

On Sunday night June 30th as she sat in the striped rocking chair in front of the stairs opposite me on the sofa, Rochester appeared behind her coming down the steps. It was only a brief moment that I saw him there slightly above Barbie, then he disappeared. My heart pounded but I said nothing. I was overjoyed! Later before she left New England I would tell her, and she both questioned and then accepted.

On July 1st before she left she sat in her same chair overlooking the gardens and lake and wrote a poem. It is so meaningful to me that I wish to include it. It speaks of the peace and serenity of life here that is ours, and that she also has experienced since she was a young girl, and that Rochester has always known and loved and shares forever with us.

VISITING NEW HAMPSHIRE

The sun is shining brightly,
The birds are chirping lightly—
Branches softly sway, as breezes
    pass, throughout the day.

The air is warm and mild,
Awakening each sense—
Providing peace and pleasure,
Instead of feeling tense.

The lake is blue and still—
Lapping gently on the sand—
It's beauty can be seen and heard,
When on surrounding land.

A place that's so serene,
And wonderful to be—

A place alive with green,
Brings happiness to me.

Barbara Jan Frances Egan
July 1, 2002

Saturday, July 20, 2002

*I*T IS ESPECIALLY POIGNANT that Barbie should come here to give me her company that I love so, and to restore her own self, and to write such a poem expressing her love of being here, only to have her own dear cat go to Heaven shortly after she returned home. She, and husband Francis, whom I have written about earlier and who made the wooden image of Rochester, now deeply grieve for their beloved twenty-one-year-old cat Gus. Gus is a sweet black and white female most precious. She too has made trips to New Hampshire when she was younger and before Rochester came into my life, and now awaits them in Heaven. Without intruding I am trying to be supportive of Barbara and Frank in ways that I have discovered, as the days pass. They too need their privacy and are helping their other cat Buddy in his grieving.

In every vision appearance Rochester has made since March 8th he has been alone in the places he enjoys in this cottage. In the vision of him with Barbie I would learn later in prayer, after Gus's passing, that *"his standing behind her"* was indicating heavenly support.

In the weeks preceding Rochester's passing as I have written earlier, I was given an insatiable desire to pray the Rosary multiple times daily. I then later learned it was a preparation for our mystical connection, Rochester's and mine through Mary, after Rochester went to Heaven. This desire for the Rosary was a sign given but that I could not recognize *before* Rochester left, just as I did not recognize Rochester's sign to Barbie and me *before* Gus's passing nor did he reveal it then.

Yet, the day before Rochester left me, March 7th, he told me in words I wrote down then and have shared with you in this journal, and will again now—*"I will enter you in a way you could never dream and this bond is eternal."* He had told me what would happen but I could not understand then. I had only to obey what was said to me within, as I stood holding his precious being in that Veterinarian's office that next day, March 8th. He trusted me to know and obey, that is how close and one we were and are.

I have not yet told Barbara what I have just written now in this journal. I will wait until I am shown it is the right time.

It is all mystery. One has to be open and receptive , live expectantly, and in perfect timing not known to us, we shall be shown what heavenly secrets we are to know. Some are painful and some are wondrous, and all are sacred.

We do not own this life, this body—
our shadows pass across the earth,
following the wind into the wide, eternal sky.
　　　　　　　　　　　　　　　　—inspired by Mexican Poetry

Everything can be borne, if we keep heaven in view.
　　　　　　　　　　　　—Ptolemy Tompkins, staff editor, *Angels on Earth*

Postscript 2

. . . the human involved must have understanding of the Divinity
within all life which innately relates each of us to every living thing
and every living thing to us—in true kinship.
—J. Allen Boone, *Kinship with All Life*

Sunday, July 21, 2002

SEVERAL HOURS AFTER WRITING THE INTRODUCTION to my book *Journal of Love: Spiritual Communication with Animals Through Journal Writing*, I overwhelmingly received a blessing. As we sat down to relax and put on the television, the screen lit up with the beginning title and credits for the old and wonderful movie of *Dr. Doolittle* starring Rex Harrison. It left me weak in wonder that this should appear, and at the very beginning of the movie so that we could view it from beginning to end. At that time we had not seen it for several years nor had we seen it listed in that time, though it may have been, but not for our eyes. I had planned to get out the video we had taped when last we viewed it and watch it again while wrapping Christmas gifts that next day, in light of what I had completed writing in the Introduction of *Journal of Love*.

The above I wrote in that book as a Postscript to that Introduction, and I believe the showing of this movie at that very moment was truly an Angelic synchronism and blessing to encourage me in what I had written, and a blessing upon the book also. (It is also blessed by having a picture of Rochester on the cover.) We discovered after viewing it, it was not listed in the TV Guide. I was, and am, deeply grateful to my Angels.

Knowing then what I have just shared from my previous book, imagine the awe I experienced when after completing the first, and what I thought would be the only "*Postscript*" to this journal, we turned on Ted Koppel's *Nightline* that evening, a favorite of ours, to experience another synchronism! The subject to be viewed and discussed was "*Corridors!*" When had we ever before seen a program on "*Corridors?*" Never! These *Corridors* were being created by a group of men; individuals and well known executives, and very especially actor Harrison Ford. (Another "*Harrison*"—but this time not Rex!!) Amazing! These *Corridors* are "*passages*" (these words were used interchangeably in the discussions) that extend from Alaska to the tip of South America, all natural land in forests and jungles and currently existing National Parks. This project is being pursued by wealthy and powerful people who are trying to arrange the purchase of, or convince countries to set aside, large parts of their territory. The goal? To have an uninterrupted corridor of land from the tip of South America to the frozen edges of North America. They have to work with governments, various agencies, and individuals. It is an enormous undertaking. The areas where negotiations are being attempted at the present time cover an area that is four times the size of California. Even this massive amount of land is only a portion of what they hope the final size will be.

And why was such an amazing project embarked upon and in such love and enthusiasm? It is for the sake of the animals in all these areas! *Animals!* They are hoping that in creating these *Corridors*, that wildlife will be saved and not become extinct. Since land elsewhere is being taken from the wildlife, and their habitats often stripped and citified, this enormous passage of land they are buying will, in its natural form as God intended, insure the protection of the wild animals, so that they may live out their natural life times in surroundings that they are meant to be in, and where their food supplies are and their families and companions. That all these men initiated such a moving and deeply caring project so that the animals may live and future generations of humans may always have these wondrous creatures in the world with them, is an act of unselfish and undying love. I want to continually learn more of this project.

Learning of it the night I finished the first "*Postscript*" to this journal, confirmed that I had chosen the correct title for this book. I had been undecided between two titles almost until completion of it, then after prayer knew it must be *In Corridors of Eternal Time—A Passage Through Grief.* And too, *A Journal.*

And now still yet another synchronism to say this *is* the correct title, for this program on *Corridors* was aired on a Friday evening, and all Friday evenings are Holy to me because of Rochester.

As I have been traveling through my *Corridor* with Rochester, a dear *animal* in a *passage* through *grief* that will end in eternity, and writing a *journal,* which is like a written *journey* on paper as compared to an actual one on land, marvelous things were being done in the world. These men are attempting to insure that unnecessary *grief* will not ever have to be if these wild animals follow these *passages* and can *journey* in their *corridors of eternal time.*

A very precious little *animal* named Rochester has already *journeyed* through his *passage* and *corridor* accompanied by Angels, and awaits me in *eternal time.* I feel certain I was mysteriously led to select the correct title for our *journal.* He knew I would be watching *Nightline.* We always view it together—holding hands.

What greater gift than the love of my cat.

—Charles Dickens

Make visible what, without you, might perhaps never have been seen.

—Robert Bresson

I pray I have made visible to you in the writing of this journal, what might never have been seen without Rochester's presence and guidance.

Thank you, and God Bless You—
and all your dear animals.

Heartbeat

Doubt that the stars are fire;
Doubt that the sun doth move;
Doubt truth to be a liar;
But never doubt I love.

—William Shakespeare

Thursday, August 29, 2002

THOUGH THIS JOURNAL OF ROCHESTER'S AND MINE shall be written and go on as long as I am alive and on earth, this segment of it was to end now. Or so I thought and planned. But something unexplainable has been happening in my life, unexplainable that is until now. And now that I have been shown the answer I too have learned in prayer I am to speak of it in this Journal. Often mystical things occur in people's lives and if we feel led to share we sometimes help another who needs an explanation for a happening in their life also. It may not be identical to what you have experienced and revealed, but it will give courage to another not to doubt their own personal experience. It is so easy to doubt when extraordinary things happen, when a phenomenon breaks through into ordinary living. We do not have to share our experiences and I kept this one of mine out of this Journal until now, but when indicated then we should speak out. I have kept many occurrences in my spiritual life to myself, but there have been others that I was led to speak and write about, and though I knew I might be criticized or thought truly strange, (and both those things did happen within my family) I followed the Holy Spirit's leading and revealed the matter in order to help others and myself. And each time it truly did help others!

As so often happens I receive a confirmation *after* I have taken a first step of boldness to speak or to act, just as I have received one this time. In this case I picked up a new book I have had waiting here to read but have left it unread due to my spiritual books I need to read in these months about grieving and dear animals. I opened this waiting book at random and on the page saw the following words indented. They read:

> When there is a profound revelation, in the very recognition that "this is revelation," you have to become serious about your own life. The instant you recognize that you are seeing the truth as it is, you must realize the implications of what is being revealed to you.

The author goes on to say that your confidence in that revelation can only grow stronger if it is not betrayed even once. He states that the stronger the confidence, then the deeper will be your wisdom. But he warns that if you carelessly or needlessly engage in or allow yourself to indulge in doubt, then your confidence will be undermined for you are walking down a precarious road. The author of these words is Andrew Cohen from his book, *Enlightenment Is a Secret*. I am not familiar with this writer but the statement appears in a book by an author that I have read and heard speak on Maine Public Television, Dr. Wayne W. Dyer. This statement is in his book, *Your Sacred Self*, which I shall eventually read. At this point in time the book was meant to give me these important words of confidence so that I might write my secret. And so I shall.

Some months before Rochester went to Heaven I began to hear an unusual thing. I cannot pinpoint when it first began but surely about a year ago, six months or so before Rochester physically left. It was like a drum beat, the soft type made on the drum of a Native American, not the type in a musical jazz group. It was steady and constant. At times it was loud, other times quite soft, but always there. It was outside not inside our home. I would wake to it every morning as the beat came in through the open windows, and then it was quite loud. I would fall asleep to it at night in that same depth of sound. The rest of the day it was always there. Often I would totally forget about it, but other times I would stand on the front porch and listen and wonder. As I write now it is beating steadily, never stopping. It has not ever stopped. I am writing outdoors on our screened in porch facing the lake. It is out there, over and over. I have been listening all these months since this time last year, and just accepting.

I not only hear it here on our property, but everywhere we go. The beat goes on when we visit family in Rhode Island, and when we go shopping in Maine every two weeks or so. It is not confined to this woods and lake of New Hampshire.

I would ask Bob if he heard this beat and always he said "*no.*" It would be loud and constant, and he would sit there and look at me and laugh and say he did not hear a thing. Knowing his nature and that he likes to tease, I definitely thought he was "*gaslighting*" me as he likes to do, or else he was losing his hearing. It often brought me to tears when he kept saying "*no*" over these past months when I was standing there hearing it just as I was hearing his very voice. Gently, and recently questioning three others close to me who did not hear it either when it was so obvious as we stood outdoors near the lake, I put it to rest. I realized no one else heard it but myself. And I thought, "*Why?!*" With one final attempt to see if Bob heard it before I came to this conclusion, I asked him to please stop the car on the wooded road we travel in Maine, and to turn off the motor and listen. With no one around and only the gentle persistent pounding beat, I listened. He heard nothing.

And then, when I finally gave up and felt total defeat, at home I sat in my prayer chair admittedly with tears, and too some thought that beside the usual things I am often teased about, that there truly must be something wrong with me. In spirit and prayer I asked Rochester if the beat had to do with him.

Rochester began to whisper to me then in spirit, and I grabbed my steno pad and green pen resting on the arm of my Adirondack prayer chair and my hand raced as I wrote the message. The message began:

Yes, it is my heartbeat. It was given to you before I left to prepare you. It is yours forever.

He went on to say other words with great love and affection, and said too that this beat is one of the many mysteries in our love. Just as I was given the incomprehensible gift of his "*Anima*" the night he went to

Heaven, so too I have been given this ability to hear his heart beat in love for me. He said in this message that he has been waiting for me to realize it, but in my grief I did not, until now. And he said with endearments *"Oh, how can you ever not be with me? You are always with me and I am always with you! Our hearts beat as one. We are one heart, one soul."* It was then he told me that it is our one heart beating in great love that I hear day and night.

There is nothing more I can say in relation to the revelation of this great love and mystical gift. To hear this *"heartbeat"* of our one heart forever is a gift so divine and unfathomable! I stand on the deck and hear it beating through the trees and over the lake and just cry.

Apparently I cannot prove it to anyone unless I am sent someone who hears it also. I know my own truth in this and Rochester's. I do not need to prove it. I place my fingers on my wrist and my heartbeat is *one* with the heartbeat of Rochester's in the ether. We are one.

And so I say to you once again and perhaps in different words, but I beg you to be open to your animal companions's great love for you and be a listener as well as a talker. Learn to listen and to write down what you hear in spirit that he/she is saying, whether he/she is still with you on earth or if he/she is in Heaven. Do not doubt!

When you recognize doubt arising in you say *no* to it and refuse to let the negative thought in your life. Detach yourself from doubt and let it dissipate. Get rid of your old thinking habits and acquire new ones that allow for occurrences that are not always explainable, and realize that God is at work. *"Doubt not only inhibits your sacred quest but can also be a destructive force in your daily existence,"* states Dr. Wayne Dyer. In the past I have always acknowledged and accepted things that I believed to be true when all around me said the opposite. And since Rochester has gone to Heaven I have received and acknowledged with great awe, gratefulness and joy his gift of *Anima* given to me March 8th (his gift of breath and soul), his vision seen by Chris in the ring of *Angels and Light*, the circle of love of the Rosary, and the *Gift of Tears*. Too, his gifts of presence and especially the intense heat when he lies upon my legs, his appearances in this cottage and in dreams, and his guidance and so much more. I surely will stand eternally firm on this gift of *"Heartbeat!"* Rochester only speaks the truth.

Reread words I have said and written here please, and in other parts of this Journal, and please do not doubt. Open your heart and mind prayerfully. Please reread the quotation I included earlier in this entry and too, please read my *Journal of Love,* or Sonya Fitzpatrick's book also mentioned. But do not doubt. Do not lose confidence in what is given to you.

If someone wants to argue with you and claims they are right, just be still and do not engage in conflict. Let it go. You know in your own heart what you have been given. Wrap it in a spiritual blanket of love and be still. Actually pause in prayer and mentally envision wrapping your truth in a soft blanket of your favorite color. The controversy will pass when there is no one present who wishes to argue or defend their truth. You do not have to defend it! Then the deeper your faith and wisdom , and the deeper your knowledge, too, with great love, will be your deeper connection to your beloved animal companion or human.

There is a verse in scripture that has had great meaning to me through the years that I previously shared in my Journal entry of Sunday, April 7th, "Forever Together." As I go through the days now I can only claim it anew and believe it with all my heart in regard to Rochester, for I know without a doubt that my hope of being with him forever in Heaven will be fulfilled. Perhaps it will strengthen and help each reader also to have it entered here again.

> *What is faith? It is the confident assurance that something we want is going to happen. It is the certainty that what we hope for is waiting for us, even though we cannot see it up ahead.*
> —Hebrews 11:1

I leave you now with this significant quotation that also appears in the beginning of our Journal.

> *In the essential of what they meant to us, the dead live on with us as long as we ourselves live. Sometimes we can speak to them and take counsel of them more readily than with the living.*
> —Hermann Hesse, author of *Siddhartha* and many other books.

Rediscovering
an Earth Angel

There is nothing permanent about earth angels.
They are rediscovered in each instant.

Things from the present and the past communicate with one another.
Thoughts fly from the present into the past and vice versa.
Imagination is the vehicle of exchange,
and images are the intermediaries who pass between worlds.
—Shaun McNiff, *Earth Angels*

Later in the evening,
Thursday, August 29, 2002

I CANNOT END THIS DAY without an additional Journal entry, for what occurred about 6:15 PM this evening needs to be written. As I finished a period of prayer in my writing room, I felt impressed to go to the back room that is opposite my writing room on the other side of the stair landing, for I needed some paper. It is on this landing I had seen and held Rochester in a very vivid dream. For a week or more I had been looking for an object connected to Rochester but had not found it. I was completely free of thoughts about this object however, before or when entering the room. As I came through the door, even though there are many books and supplies and other related objects in the room, my eyes fell immediately on a little purple flowered zippered purse. Though I go in and out of this room several times a day, in all these months I never saw this purple purse. It is one of the side effects of grief, not being as observing along with chinks in my memory.

An incident had occurred over a week ago in the family that had been reported to us from afar, and it brought back pain that had existed for many years. At one point in my life in Pennsylvania in early June of 1986 that I have related before, the pain was such that I had no desire to live for there seemed to be no answer to it all. Within a couple weeks following that, June 23, God set Rochester down in that Mall in Rochester, New Hampshire. He sent me an Angel! Through all the difficult times that followed through the years due to this situation, Rochester was ever with me giving me his undying love, constant companionship, gentleness, and so much more. During an especially hard time in relation to this in 1987, I was purchasing a gift that I was having engraved for a friend. While waiting at the counter in Sears as the gift was being personalized, and through misty eyes while thinking of this unsolvable problem, I saw a small shiny brass cat on display under the glass. It resembled Rochester! When my first purchase was handed to me completed I asked to see the cat. It was a key chain. I returned it to the salesman and asked for an engraving on the back of it. I requested the words *"Rochester Loves Me."* I knew with all my heart Rochester loved me so much, but at that point in time I could be certain of no one else's love. I treasured that little key chain and always kept it in the little purple flowered purse within the larger shoulder bag I carried. We would travel back and forth to New Hampshire for years before moving here permanently in 1996, so my shoulder bag was always attached to me it seemed whether while I was on the road or on errands around town in Pennsylvania. I felt Rochester's love always and the little key chain image of him was an added touch. Once we moved here permanently the little purple purse laid on my big desk where Rochester himself often laid too when not on his comforter or my lap as I wrote all day.

But several weeks before Chester went to Heaven our daughter Barbara came to visit. I straightened up my writing room where she always stays, and tidied up my desk. I placed some objects that held meaning in a small box in order to give Barbie more space and carried them to the back room. When she left, Rochester went to Heaven very shortly after. In all these months I never reclaimed the personal items in that box and brought them back to their special places on my desk. I forgot they existed. How could I have forgotten that dear brass image of Rochester that said those precious words?!

But as I have written at the beginning of this entry, for a week or more I had been looking for this very object connected to Rochester but had not found it. When I walked in that back room today after prayer, I had been tearful over the recent family incident and the overwhelming feeling of Chester's physical absence. His presence had always been there for me, his precious soft body to hold and cuddle with, his soft paws and dear golden eyes that gave me such love and comfort in all of life and especially in difficult times. And at this moment I saw the purple flowered purse. I picked it up and went back to our writing room. I still did not remember its contents. It had been almost six months since I placed it there and then life totally changed.

When I sat down and looked within, there was the brass image of Rochester encircled by two Rosaries that I do not even remember seeing before in my life! I had never kept a rosary in this purse with the image of Chester! Only his image was kept in there! I cannot explain the joy and awe I felt as I lifted out the image of Chester from the purse and kissed its face and then read the back. *"Rochester Loves You."* I dissolved into tears. I needed to see that so badly even though I always know it. How I wish I had remembered it so I could have carried it with me here in this cottage and every where I went since March 8th! A simple material object that had brought such comfort surfaced at a time when Rochester knew I needed it. It was an *Earth Angel!* Rochester knew that term too. We wrote about it in *Journal of Love.* Only he could have drawn my attention to it that very moment and I was receptive. Perhaps he had tried many times before these past months, but I simply could not see as I once did. My heart is so heavy. He never relayed it in any messages I wrote down from him. There were too many other important words to be said to each other, and he always tells his precious love for me. I do not know why it occurred this particular day and not another, but I know it was only because of Rochester.

And to have two strange rosaries encircling it just as Mary's rosaries and prayers have been encircling us these past months, is unfathomable! There are mysteries that defy explanation! And that the prayers recited when praying the Rosary are called *"mysteries,"* only emphasizes this.

I came downstairs overjoyed and in tears after praying a decade on one of the rosaries for Rochester and myself. I chose the one that seemed most significant, for the beads were divided in color. Some were green and some violet, or purple. And these are Rochester's and my favorite colors! I had never seen this Rosary before, nor the tan one. Even tan is an unusual shade for a Rosary. .And if all this was not gift and consolation enough, I immediately found a green marbleized copy book of mine that too had been misplaced. I particularly wanted it because there was a sketch of Rochester I had made on one of the pages. As he laid on my legs one night in bed I had drawn a picture of him in sleep. I had hoped to include it in this Journal, and now I can. A copy of it made for me by Bob will appear with the poem "Understanding" in the Journal entries under "Angels and Stars."

As I have been writing here about the rosaries, unexpectedly I was reminded of other roses, that like my rosaries, contain *mysteries*.

Some weeks ago when in Maine I went down the aisle of a store we shop in that displayed only ceramic ware, vases, art objects and small statues. I was just passing through to go elsewhere but at the end of the aisle was a bright spot of pink on the right side. When I arrived there I found a lovely bouquet of pink silk roses that contained five large full blooms and two buds. They were totally out of place on this aisle. There were no other flowers at all. But they just touched my heart and I took them. There was no price tag on them like other articles for sale so the check-out person created a price that was so low that they were almost complimentary. At home I placed them outside on the screened in porch on a table with my live Jade plants and have been appreciating them each day. I bought them for Rochester for he always loved real flowers and these were very lifelike.

After enjoying them these past weeks I read in a spiritual book that pink roses are a way that our loved ones in Heaven often express love to us. Because it is a mystery, there is no explanation as to how they appear when they do, but they are a gift from a beloved one. This just over-whelmed me, for I believe it, and I had bought the roses for Rochester that mysteriously, like a mystery in the Rosary, brought me comfort to do so for him.

Yet the pink roses had mysteriously been placed there in a store I shop in every two weeks or so on an aisle that had no other flowers

242 soo In Corridors of Eternal Time

displayed, and had no price tag attached to them, for me from Rochester, if I am to accept this explanation. I have accepted it.

Roses and their scent subtly and mysteriously detected, are connected to our Blessed Mother Mary, and continuously I pray her Rosary for Rochester. My Rosary was with me when these pink roses awaited me. What I believed I was giving as a gift to Rochester, Rochester had arranged for me to find from him. Perhaps you wonder that I believe it, but all of living is a mystery now and I cannot reject something so tender and beautiful associated with Mary and Rochester. I need such mysteries as I travel this passage. We all need such mysteries.

I have had two more dreams also of Rochester in recent nights, and two others previous to those. Always they are dreams of things he did and does in everyday life here. In both recent dreams he was on our screened in porch standing on the blue carpet between the kitchen door where I was standing in the dream looking out at him, and the door of the porch. His right side was toward me. It was a scene that took place many times in real life. He was in almost the identical spot and stance in both dreams that occurred consecutive nights. He is ever telling me and showing me he is always here with me. It is consoling beyond words.

Last Friday evening following my Holy hour of prayer with Rochester that had extended past 6:00 PM, I turned the small lamp on by the chair I sit in to pray. I wanted to meditate and talk to Chester because I was still so sad and teary. As I sat in the silence doing this with my eyes closed, suddenly there was flickering of light through my eye lids. I remained still, eyes tightly closed, and allowed myself to experience this. I thought it strange, though am growing accustomed with eternal gratitude for the very unusual and new happenings in my life since Rochester is here continually in spirit. The light continued to flicker. I finally opened my eyes. It had been doing this continuously for seven minutes (I knew when I began to meditate), but when I opened my eyes it did it only for a few seconds and stopped. In my heart I knew it was Rochester sending me his love. I tried the light bulb and it was tight and secure. This is our room where we shared life and I believe it was Chester consoling me as I sat with wet eyes. My bulb never did that before. I believe In my heart he was simply assuring me he is always with me. I refuse to doubt gifts I am given. Chester was always a light to me, a precious, shining Angel and Star.

I have had a day once again filled with Rochester's presence and abiding love. It was too extraordinary not to include in this personal Journal. This is the way life is lived with my precious feline companion, both before March 8th and ever after. He is with me always and he continuously makes me aware of his eternal companionship. If only I could hold his warm little body in my arms and kiss his precious face. Someday I shall again. Until that day I do it continuously in spirit.

Now, or thirty years from now, is a speck in this thing called eternity.
—Dr. Wayne W. Dyer

Sometimes we are forced to be apart from what we desire. At these difficult times the Angels are always near us to help us grow stronger in patience, faith and trust.
—Shaun McNiff, *Earth Angels*

In the beginning—tiny Rochester even then fascinated with the light of the television and, too, the pictures

A Final Thought

Friday, August 30, 2002

*A*FTER WRITING MY INTRODUCTION TO THIS JOURNAL and while doing the proofreading, I received a blessing out of the blue. On this day Friday morning, August 30, an e-mail came to me from a woman, a stranger, from the United Kingdom. Upon reading her message I just dissolved into tears and carried it around with me for the next hour. I then answered briefly, with much gratitude telling her I would respond more fully very shortly. I simply could not respond to it all in my first reply because it affected me so deeply. Too, that this message had come from so far away was very meaningful, and that she would take the time to write to me. Knowing anew Rochester was touching lives was an unfathomable gift.

The fact that Alison first sent me this e-mail on *August 21st,* the anniversary of my Dad's entering Heaven, and that it is he whom I have asked to take care of Rochester—was the first sign it was a blessing. It was returned to her because my e-mail address had been changed since it first appeared in my book that she had, and she re-sent it. It arrived today, a Friday, Rochester's and my Holy Day. All of this has so much significance to me. The main reason she wrote was to tell me how much my book, *Journal of Love—Spiritual Communication with Animals Through Writing,* means to her, and her beautiful message contained many thoughts and responses to this. She had just completed reading it. She said loving and kind words about Rochester, and that she too has been a vegetarian for 14 years. She specifically mentioned a page she loved in the book, page 5, which expresses my spiritual beliefs and philosophy in regard to animals and communication with them. She said too she felt the wonderful energy of Rochester and my prayer chair and platform by the lake. It is such a blessing to receive this today and will always bless me.

I pray each night that I will experience Rochester anew as each day breaks, and I do experience him. But I say special prayers for *"Fridays"* because each one is so significant and painful. Without a doubt I believe this letter is a gift from Rochester as he inspires Alison through the reading of his book and mine, and then to lead her to write to me. After all, *he taught me* to communicate *with him* through writing!

Alison's words that I include here, perhaps will help you who read this Journal of Rochester's and mine, to realize that our beloved animal companions *can communicate with us*—even from the pages of a book to a woman across the sea, and after passing. Our animal companions *are forever with us.*

Alison writes:

I have found your book to have such a wonderfully spiritually and uplifting vibration throughout. It is a very special book and I certainly feel you were most courageous in writing it and having it published.

She is a therapist and practices Reiki, and her words are so affirming and confirming to me. I can never doubt what I am experiencing or what I have written in this Journal, or my previous *Journal of Love.*

Another loving woman from England who now resides in the United States, Sonya Fitzpatrick, has also stated these beliefs about animal communication and on national television. She often says, *"Animals are forever."*

Rochester and I say: O yes, and Amen!

Wednesday, September 4, 2002

*A*GAIN TODAY I RECEIVE ANOTHER LONG E-MAIL from Alison from the United Kingdom. I had answered her previous one responding to all that she wrote, then told her of Rochester's passing. Too, I told her briefly of how he is ever with me in ways written about extensively in this Journal. She said how sorry she is to learn that Rochester has passed and said "*The depth of your relationship came through clearly in the book and I understand that you must be inconsolable to have lost such a close and loving companion.*" She too wrote that it must be harder to bear because our relationship was so unique, between human and cat.

In ending her latest message to me she gave me a poem she had discovered on an Angel web site that I would like to give to you. Too, I leave you with Alison's own closing words. That a stranger could write such inspired words about my Rochester can only emphasize and impart all that I have attempted to share with you about this precious, loving, Angel creature that shares life with me, and with whom I shall share eternity. I am so appreciative for Alison's message.

> The tide recedes but leaves behind
> bright seashells on the sand,
> The sun goes down, but gentle warmth
> still lingers on the land,
> The music stops, and yet
> it echoes on in sweet refrains.
> For every joy that passes,
> Something beautiful remains.

Alison writes:

> And that something is a beautiful soul called Rochester, who leaves behind him a legacy of wisdom and knowledge that will reach the hearts of many and guide them further along their spiritual path—a gift of inestimable value.
>
> Thank you, dear, kind, wise Rochester, who has graced this earth with his presence and left it all the richer for his stay."

Any correspondence to the author of this book may be addressed to:
Janice Gray Kolb
Post Office Box #5
East Wakefield, NH 03830
Jan@JaniceGrayKolb.com

"ROCHESTER"
T. PETERSON 7/03

Thursday, July 17, 2003

$\mathcal{A}$S I COMPLETE THIS BOOK'S FINAL PROOFREADING this day for my publisher before it is about to be printed, I receive a package in the mail. It is from my new friend in Colorado, Sue Peterson. In January when this book was accepted for publication I also met Sue at that time via e-mail. Rochester introduced us through our book, *Journal of Love*, which Sue had ordered and read. When she wrote me in response to it, a unique correspondence began. She too loves animals, and she and her husband Tom have numerous animal companions, and I am fortunate to now have sweet pictures of them all. Sue went on to read other books of mine that also have Rochester in them, but it was *Journal of Love* that initiated our friendship.

As I have written throughout this book, Rochester is a gift to me and he has also bestowed many gifts on me in his physical lifetime and in his life in spirit here with me. Today as I complete the final proofreading, I open the package from Sue after making myself wait two hours to do so.

I sense that what is within is significant, and I need to appreciate its mysterious presence first unseen.

At last I lift out the gift within and simply dissolve. I hold it to me and cannot believe that two people I have never met would be so loving as to do this.

In my embrace is a 5x7 portrait of Rochester in the medium of a pencil drawing done by Sue's husband Tom. It is completely life-like and Rochester's beautiful large eyes look deeply into mine. It is as if he is once again and ever saying, "I am here." Even his pewter St. Francis medal is in detail about his neck and he is within a handsome brown frame with a thin geometrical design toward the inner edge. That he should inspire my new friends to create such a gift for me reveals anew what I have been trying to continually express. He is an Angel and he is ever with me. For this portrait to have been created by a loving man I have never met indicates the power of love and inspiration my Rochester causes to emanate to others. How precious that Tom Peterson should be inspired and make the time to draw this life-like icon of Rochester that arrives on the very day that Rochester's book, *In Corridors of Eternal Time*, is finalized. It is a keepsake of love from my little beloved Angel and eternal companion through Tom and Sue Peterson and their love and kindness. Thank you, thank you.

I share Tom and Sue's gift here with you to bless you too.

A Place in Eternity

Robert A. Kolb, Jr.

(1) There is a place in e-ter-ni-ty where I'll wor-ship at my
(2) The days are few from our mor-tal birth that we walk with God on His
(3) Be strong my faith— don't hes-i-tate. — For we know not when that

Master's knee, sur-roun-ded by His heaven-ly grace I'll look up-on His
sweet green earth, but in cor-ri-dors of e-ter-nal time joy with Him will be sub-
awesome date. When our earthly deeds are ac-coun-ted for as we pass the heaven-ly

Chorous

face.
lime. When my work here has ended — I'll at last be there
door.

too. — For His prom-ise to join Him in the — I know to be true.
church triumphant

I thought I could describe a state; make a map of sorrow. Sorrow, however, turns out to be not a state, but a process. It needs not a map but a history, and if I don't stop writing that history at some quite arbitrary point, there's no reason why I should ever stop. There is something new to be chronicled every day. Grief is like a long valley where any bend may reveal a totally new landscape. Not every bend does. Sometimes the surprise is the opposite one; you are presented with exactly the same sort of country you thought you left behind miles ago.

—C.S. Lewis, *A Grief Observed*

Janice Kolb along with her husband Bob are the parents of six grown children and have nineteen grandchildren. Their life has revolved around raising a loving family with religious values. In addition to raising their family, Janice developed a letter writing and audio tape ministry that gives encouragement and spiritual support to those who need it all over the United States.

Other inspirational works published by Janice Kolb include: *Journal of Love, Compassion for All Creatures, Higher Ground, The Enchantment of Writing, Beneath the Stars and Trees . . . there is a place, Beside the Still Waters,* and *The Pine Cone Journal.* In a cooperative effort, Janice wrote the book, *Whispered Notes,* with her husband Bob.

Also by Janice Kolb

Journal of Love
Spiritual Communication with Animals Through Journal Writing
ISBN: 1-57733-046-3, 180 pp., 30 illus., $14.95

"Animal whisperer" Janice Kolb shares her heart-lifting journey of discovery as she learns to communicate with her beloved feline companion, Rochester—first by using her intuition and then by writing a journal of their "conversations."

*"Once again the delightful and insightful Jan Kolb has provided all of us who truly love animals with another warm and wonderful book about how we may enter into deeper communication with our beloved pets. **Journal of Love** is destined to become a classic in the field of transpecies communication."*
—Brad Steiger and Sherry Hansen Steiger, authors of *Animal Miracles*

Compassion for All Creatures
An Inspirational Guide for Healing the Ostrich Syndrome
ISBN: 1-57733-008-0, 264 pp., 47 illus., $12.95

A very personal book of experiences, confessions, and deep thoughts praising all God's creatures through photos, poems and meditations. This book lends an impassioned voice for examining animal rights from Mother Nature's point of view.

"Jan Kolb has written a very special book that will surprise you in many ways. Learning compassion and reverence by way of the animal kingdom makes perfect sense. She ponders deep questions and important issues which inspire her passion for all of life. Whether or not you join her crusade for the animal kingdom, you will end up thinking, and awareness leads to change."
—Terry Lynn Taylor, author of *Messengers of Light*

Blue Dolphin Publishing • 800-643-0765 • www.bluedolphinpublishing.com

The Enchantment of Writing
Spiritual Healing and Delight
Through the Written Word
ISBN: 1-57733-073-0, 312 pp., 48 illus., $14.95

Janice Kolb shares events from her life that illustrate how to train yourself to write daily. Her encouragement and guidance for writing lead naturally to self-discovery. By preserving your thoughts and experiences, you discover new sources of guidance and insight.

"There are angels cheering for us when we lift up our pens, because they know we want to do it. In this torrential moment we have decided to change the energy of the world. We are going to write down what we think. Right or wrong doesn't matter. We are standing up and saying who we are."
—Natalie Goldberg from *Wild Mind*

Higher Ground
ISBN: 1-57733-071-4, 176 pp., 16 illus., $14.95

Written freely, and from the heart, *Higher Ground* is a small treasure reserved for those who retreat into the silence and who wish to renew their purpose for living. It chronicles the experiences and thoughts of a woman on retreat in the woods of New Hampshire as she deals with personal fears and family problems and shares her faith.

From the book: *Like Thoreau—I went to the woods to be alone. Always this had been a dream—to stay by myself in our cottage in New Hampshire. Now that time had come. Depression and sadness had been settling in on me for too many months due to personal and family concerns. Each day's existence had become a hardship. My eyes filled with tears at unexpected moments. Though never intended, there were often times when I would sit for a minute to try to get myself together only to find later I had been there immobile for an extended period. Everything mattered intensely yet nothing mattered at all. The smallest chore was too big. Merely trying to begin anything was such an effort that I frequently just gave up completely....*

Blue Dolphin Publishing • 800-643-0765 • www.bluedolphinpublishing.com

Beneath the Stars & Trees ...
there is a place
A Woodland Retreat

ISBN: 1-57733-106-0, 372 pp., 47 illus., $16.95

Beneath the Stars & Trees will help you withdraw from life's distractions and retreat to a place where you can see clearly the multitude of complex factors that make up your life. Share in thoughts and experiences which can open your mind to a world of peace and new possibilities for your life.

"*Join Janice Kolb in a sometimes quirky, always perky, jaunt through lake-in-the-woods living, full of shapeshifting and kitty-cat angels, touching journal entries and frolicking poems, prayer chairs and little gnome tea parties—plus a spiritual encounter with a moose you're sure to remember forever.*"
—Michael Burnham, writer/journalist

"*Jan's Woodland Retreat is a place teeming with animal and human life, and yet peaceful and serene. It is a perfect place to meditate, reflect, and renew your spirit. Beneath the stars and trees, there truly is a special place, and Jan's book will transport you there, as often as you wish.*"
—Mark Sardella, columnist, *The Wakefield Daily Item*

Beside the Still Waters
Creative Meditations from the Woods

ISBN: 1-57733-122-2, 276 pp., 11 illus., $16.95

Beside the Still Waters is a personal view of prayer. Jan suggests a variety of ways to be in constant contact with God. These meditations can transform your prayer life into a source of personal fulfillment, power and strength. Many of these prayers may be familiar; others may be new to you. Being open to all that you read, you may discover new pathways to God and loving consolation. Though written from a Christian perspective, these prayers can be adapted to other traditions.

Blue Dolphin Publishing • 800-643-0765 • www.bluedolphinpublishing.com

Printed in the United States
18848LVS00002B/143